Ch. 1+2
120-175
184-196
212-219

A Black
Theology
of Liberation

Also by James H. Cone
Black Theology and Black Power

The C. Eric Lincoln Series in Black Religion

A Black Theology of Liberation by James H. Cone
Black Preaching by Henry H. Mitchell

A Black
Theology
of Liberation

JAMES H. CONE

J. B. Lippincott Company
Philadelphia & New York

ISBN–0–397–10097–3 Cloth Ed.
ISBN–0–397–10098–1 Paper Ed.
20 19 18 17 16 15 14 13 12
Printed in the United States of America
Library of Congress Catalog Card No.: 74–120333

TO MY MOTHER

and

IN MEMORY OF MY FATHER

Foreword

This series of books is about the black religious experience. It is addressed to Blackamericans because the rich heritage that is their history has not been made fully available to them in the usual ways in which a society informs its membership about the significant aspects of its development. Blackamericans want to know—indeed they *must* know—more about who they *were* and who they *are* if they are seriously concerned about whom they intend to become. The black man's religion is a critical component of his American passage from slavery to a freedom which is still to be perfected.

This series is addressed to white America, too. The black experience—religious, social, economic, political—is writ large in the cultural development of the larger society. Understanding it is crucial to an informed perspective of what America is or can become. To a degree not always recognized, America is what it is because the black minority is here, and has been here since long before this nation came into being.

The blacks brought their religion with them. After a time they accepted the white man's religion, but they have not always expressed it in the white man's way. It became the black man's purpose—perhaps it was his *destiny*—to shape, to fashion, to re-create the religion offered him by the Christian slavemaster, to remold it nearer to his own heart's desire, nearer to his own peculiar needs. The black religious experience is something more than a black patina on a white happening. It is a unique response to an historical occurrence which can never be replicated for any people in America.

The black man's pilgrimage in America was made less onerous because of his religion. His religion was the organizing principle around which his life was structured. His church was his school, his forum, his political arena, his social club, his art gallery, his conservatory of music. It was lyceum and gymnasium as well as *sanctum sanctorum*. His religion was his fellowship with man, his audience with God. It was the peculiar sustaining force which gave him the strength to endure when endurance gave no promise, and the courage to be creative in the face of his own dehumanization.

This is the black religious experience. This is what this book and this series is about.

. . . .

Revolution is the preeminent characteristic of our time. There is not one revolution; there are many. Sometimes they are tangential to each other. At other times they surge together for a while like the overflow of separate rivers at flood stage.

The Black Revolution is a critical component of a revolutionary era. It is the father of the revolutionary spirit now challenging America. The Black Revolution was first to call into question the comfortable presumptions upon which we, as a culture, staked our world view and our private identity. It was first to demand that we prove our claims to the preemptions and the prerogatives we have always taken for granted.

This book is a product of the Black Revolution. It is one book of a series concerned to make some contribution toward the documentation and the interpretation of the religious experience of black people in America. It is born of the recognition that the Blackamerican needs to know who he is religiously—no less than politically or socially—that others whose attitudes and behavior are structured by their perceptions need to know. It is an aspect of the humanistic side of the social reconstruction that is implicit in the Black Revolution.

Every revolution is addressed to the future. It is addressed to change. In a highly literate society such as ours, the quality of a revolutionary enterprise is reflected in the literature of the revolution. Revolutions begin in the mind—with the conception and the projection of an idea. They end in the mind—with the acceptance or the rejection of an idea. The literature of

what would Marx say to that?

a revolution is the best index as to whether the future to which the revolution is addressed is the future of an ideology, or whether it is the future of an illusion. The rhetoric of revolution is an aspect of activism. It is usually exciting; but it is always evanescent. The literature of revolution is the distillate of reason. It is the continuing confrontation, and it is the insistent refutation of an archaic social order, a stagnant way of looking at things.

James H. Cone, in *A Black Theology of Liberation*, makes an important contribution to the validity of the Black Revolution and to the inevitability of its success. Religion was from the beginning the organizing principle of the black experience in America. It is basic to any understanding of what Blackamericans are or of what they are determined to become. Every religion presupposes the development of a theology which explains its central meaning and gives it perspective. Professor Cone is the first theologian to give formal and systematic expression to the meaning of black religion and to place it in the context of the Black Revolution. But Dr. Cone's larger contribution transcends the Black Revolution and offers to America, and to the church, a key to understanding something more about this society and something more about the faith than we have ever undertaken to learn.

C. Eric Lincoln, Series Editor

Union Theological Seminary
New York, N.Y.

Preface

The reader is entitled to know what to expect in this book. It is my contention that Christianity is essentially a religion of liberation. The function of theology is that of analyzing the meaning of that liberation for the oppressed community so they can know that their struggle for political, social, and economic justice is consistent with the gospel of Jesus Christ. Any message that is not related to the liberation of the poor in the society is not Christ's message. Any theology that is indifferent to the theme of liberation is not Christian theology.

In a society where men are oppressed because they are *black*, Christian theology must become *Black Theology*, a theology that is unreservedly identified with the goals of the oppressed community and seeking to interpret the divine character of their struggle for liberation. "Black Theology" is a phrase that is particu-

11

larly appropriate for contemporary America because of its symbolic power to convey both what whites mean by oppression and what blacks mean by liberation. However, I am convinced that the patterns of meaning centered in the idea of Black Theology are by no means restricted to the American scene, since blackness symbolizes oppression and liberation in any society.

It will be evident, therefore, that this book is written primarily for the black community and not for white people. Whites may read it and to some degree render an intellectual analysis of it, but an authentic understanding is dependent on the blackness of their existence in the world. There will be no peace in America until white people begin to hate their whiteness, asking from the depths of their being: "How can we become black?" It is hoped that enough people will begin to ask that question that this country will no longer be divided on the basis of color. But until then, it is the task of the Christian theologian to do theology in the light of the concreteness of human oppression as expressed in color, and to interpret for the oppressed the meaning of God's liberation in their community.

This book is the result of the encouragement of many people, all of whom it would be impossible to mention. I am especially grateful to the many black people who responded so positively to my first work, *Black Theology and Black Power* (Seabury Press).

Without their encouragement, the present work would be unthinkable.

Many people read my manuscript and offered helpful criticisms. The list is much too long to mention everyone. Also, most of this material was given as lectures at several colleges and universities where insightful dialogue with students and faculty took place.

However, a special word of thanks is due to my friend William Hordern, president of the Lutheran Theological Seminary. His critical reading of the manuscript improved the manuscript considerably. Several parts of this work were rewritten after his comments, especially Chapter VII.

I am particularly indebted to Lester Scherer of Eastern Michigan University, my former colleague at Adrian College. His editorial expertise improved the manuscript immensely. Much more important is his friendship, which dates back to our seminary experience at Garrett. We both matured as we faced the reality of the Black Revolution in America and its meaning for our existence in the world.

I am grateful to C. Eric Lincoln, my colleague at Union, for the invitation to write this work for the C. Eric Lincoln Series in Black Religion. His confidence and encouragement have been invaluable to me.

My wife, Rose, and my two sons, Michael and Charles, cooperated in the bringing of this work into existence. Without the understanding patience of my family, I could not have written this work.

JAMES H. CONE

Union Theological Seminary
1970

Contents

16   *Contents*

I

The Content
of Theology

Liberation as the Content of Theology

Christian theology is a theology of liberation. It is
a rational study of the being of God in the world in
light of the existential situation of an oppressed community, relating the forces of liberation to the essence
of the gospel, which is Jesus Christ. This means that its
sole reason for existence is to put into ordered speech
the meaning of God's activity in the world, so that the
community of the oppressed will recognize that their
inner thrust for liberation is not only *consistent* with
the gospel but *is* the gospel of Jesus Christ. There can
be no Christian theology which is not identified unreservedly with those who are humiliated and abused. In
fact, theology ceases to be a theology of the gospel
when it fails to arise out of the community of the op-

pressed. For it is impossible to speak of the God of Israelite history, who is the God who revealed himself in
Jesus Christ, without recognizing that he is the God *of*
and *for* those who labor and are heavy laden.

The perspective and direction of this study are already made clear. The reader is entitled to know at the
outset what is to be defined as important. This definition and the assumptions on which it is based are to be
tested by the working out of a theology which can then
be judged according to its consistency with a community's view of the ultimate. We begin now by exploring
some preliminary considerations in our definition.

The definition of theology as that discipline which
seeks to analyze the nature of the Christian faith in the
light of the oppressed arises chiefly from the biblical
tradition itself. (1) Though it may not be entirely clear
why God elected Israel to be his people, one point is
evident: The election is inseparable from the event of
the Exodus.

> You have seen what I did to the Egyptians, and how I
> bore you on eagles' wings and brought you to myself.
> Now therefore, if you will obey my voice and keep my
> covenant, you shall be my own possession among all
> peoples. . . . (Exodus 19:4–5a)

Certainly this means, among other things, that God's
call of this people is related to their oppressed condition and to his own liberating activity already seen in
the Exodus. *You have seen what I did!* By delivering

this people from Egyptian bondage and inaugurating the covenant on the basis of that historical event, God reveals that he is the God of the oppressed, involved in their history, liberating them from human bondage.

(2) Later stages of Israelite history also show that God is particularly concerned about the oppressed within the community of Israel. The rise of Old Testament prophecy is due primarily to the lack of justice within that community. The prophets of Israel are prophets of social justice, reminding the people that Yahweh is the author of justice. It is important to note in this connection that the righteousness of God is not an abstract quality in the being of God, as with Greek philosophy. It is rather God's active involvement in history, making right what men have made wrong. The consistent theme in Israelite prophecy is Yahweh's concern for the lack of social, economic, and political justice for those who are poor and unwanted in the society. Yahweh, according to Hebrew prophecy, will not tolerate injustice against the poor; through his activity the poor will be vindicated. Again, God reveals himself as the God of liberation for the oppressed.

(3) In the New Testament, the Old Testament theme of liberation is reaffirmed by Jesus himself. The conflict with Satan and the powers, the condemnation of the rich, the insistence that the Kingdom is for the poor, and the locating of his ministry among the poor—these and other features of the career of Jesus show that his work was directed to the oppressed for the purpose of

Jesus was poor

their liberation. To suggest that he was speaking of a "spiritual" liberation fails to take seriously Jesus' thoroughly Hebrew view of man. Entering into the Kingdom of God means that Jesus himself becomes man's ultimate loyalty, for *he is the Kingdom*. This view of man's existence in the world has far-reaching implications for economic, political, and social institutions. They no longer can have ultimate claim on man's life; he is liberated and thus free to rebel against all powers that threaten man's life in the Kingdom. That is what Jesus had in mind when he said:

> The Spirit of the Lord is upon me, because he has anointed me to preach good news to the poor. He has sent me to proclaim release to the captives and recovering of sight to the blind, to set at liberty those who are oppressed, to proclaim the acceptable year of the Lord. (Luke 4:18–19)

In view of the biblical emphasis on liberation, it seems not only appropriate but necessary to define the Christian community as the community of the oppressed which joins Christ in his fight for the liberation of men. The task of theology then is to explicate the meaning of God's liberating activity so that those who labor under enslaving powers will see that the forces of liberation are the activity of God himself. Christian theology is never just a rational study of the being of God. Rather it is a study of God's liberating activity in the world, his activity on behalf of the oppressed.

If the history of Israel and the New Testament description of the historical Jesus reveal that God is a God who is identified with Israel because she is an oppressed community, the resurrection of Christ means that all oppressed peoples become his people. Herein lies the universal note implied in the gospel message of Jesus. The resurrection-event means that God's liberating work is not only for the house of Israel but for all who are enslaved by principalities and powers. The resurrection conveys hope in God. Nor is this the "hope" that promises a reward in heaven in order to ease the pain of injustice on earth. Rather it is hope which focuses on the future in order to make men refuse to tolerate present inequities. To see the future of God, as revealed in his resurrection in Christ, is to see also the contradiction of any earthly injustice with existence in Christ. That is why Camilo Torres was right when he described revolutionary action as "a Christian, a priestly struggle." [1]

The task of Christian theology, then, is to analyze the meaning of hope in God in such a way that the oppressed community of a given society will risk all for earthly freedom, a freedom made possible in the resurrection of Christ. The language of theology challenges the societal structures because it is inseparable from the suffering community. Theology can never be neu-

---

[1] Quoted in José Bonino, "Christians and the Political Revolution," in S. C. Rose and P. P. Van Lelyveld, eds., *Risk*, spec. ed., *The Development Apocalypse* 1967, p. 109.

tral or fail to take sides on issues related to the plight of the oppressed. For this reason it can never engage in conversation about the nature of God without confronting those elements of human existence which threaten man's existence as person. Whatever theology says about God and the world must arise out of its sole reason for existence as a discipline: to assist the oppressed in their liberation. Its language is always language about human liberation, proclaiming the end of bondage and interpreting the religious dimensions of the revolutionary struggle.

Liberation and Black Theology

Unfortunately, American white theology has not been involved in the struggle for black liberation. It has been basically a theology of the white oppressor, giving religious sanction to the genocide of Indians and the enslavement of black people. From the very beginning to the present day, American white theological thought has been "patriotic," either by defining the theological task independently of black suffering (the liberal northern approach) or by defining Christianity as compatible with white racism (the conservative southern approach). In both cases theology becomes a servant of the state, and that can only mean death to black people. It is little wonder that an increasing number of black religionists are finding it difficult to be black and also to be identified with traditional theological thought forms.

The appearance of Black Theology [2] on the American scene then is due exclusively to the failure of white religionists to relate the gospel of Jesus to the pain of being black in a white racist society. It arises from the need of black people to liberate themselves from white oppressors. Black Theology is a theology of liberation because it is a theology which arises from an identification with the oppressed blacks of America, seeking to interpret the gospel of Christ in the light of the black condition. It believes that the liberation of black people *is* God's liberation.

The task of Black Theology then is to analyze the nature of the gospel of Jesus Christ in the light of oppressed black people so they will see the gospel as inseparable from their humiliated condition, bestowing on them the necessary power to break the chains of oppression. This means that it is a theology of and for the black community, seeking to interpret the religious dimensions of the forces of liberation in that community.

There are two reasons why Black Theology is Christian theology and possibly the only expression of Christian theology in America. First, there can be no theology of the gospel which does not arise from an oppressed community. This is so because God in Christ has revealed himself as a God whose righteousness is inseparable

[2] See James Cone, *Black Theology and Black Power* (New York: The Seabury Press, 1969).

from the weak and helpless in human society. The goal of Black Theology is to interpret God's activity as he is related to the oppressed black community.

Second, Black Theology is Christian theology because it centers on Jesus Christ. There can be no Christian theology which does not have Jesus Christ as its point of departure. Though Black Theology affirms the black condition as the primary datum of reality which must be reckoned with, this does not mean that it denies the absolute revelation of God in Jesus Christ. Rather it affirms it. Unlike white theology which tends to make the Christ-event an abstract, intellectual idea, Black Theology believes that the black community itself is precisely where Christ is at work. The Christ-event in twentieth-century America is a black-event, that is, an event of liberation taking place in the black community in which black people recognize that it is incumbent upon them to throw off the chains of white oppression by whatever means they regard as suitable. This is what God's revelation means to black and white America, and why Black Theology may be the only possible theology in our time.

It is to be expected that some persons will ask, "Why Black Theology? Is it not true that God is color blind? Is it not true that there are others who suffer as much as, if not more in some cases than, black people?" These questions reveal a basic lack of understanding regarding Black Theology, and also a superficial view of the world at large. There are at least three points to be made here.

First, in a revolutionary situation there can never be just theology. It is always theology identified with a particular community. It is either identified with those who inflict oppression or with those who are its victims. A theology of the latter is authentic Christian theology, and a theology of the former is a theology of the Antichrist. Insofar as Black Theology is a theology arising from an identification with the oppressed black community and seeks to interpret the gospel of Jesus Christ in the light of the liberation of that community, it is Christian theology. American white theology is a theology of the Antichrist, insofar as it arises from an identification with the white community, thereby placing God's approval on white oppression of black existence.

Second, in a racist society, God is never color blind. To say God is color blind is analogous to saying that God is blind to justice and injustice, to right and wrong, to good and evil. Certainly this is not the picture of God revealed in the Old and New Testaments. Yahweh takes sides. On the one hand, he sides with Israel against the Canaanites as she makes her settlement in Palestine. On the other hand, he sides with the poor within the community of Israel against the rich and other political oppressors. In the New Testament, Jesus is not *for all,* but for the oppressed, the poor and unwanted of society, and against oppressors. The God of the biblical tradition is not uninvolved or neutral regarding human affairs; rather he is quite involved. He is active in human history, taking sides with the oppressed of the land. If God is not involved in human history, then all theology is useless, and Christianity itself is a mockery, a hollow, meaningless diversion.

The meaning of this message for our contemporary situation is clear: God, because he is a God of the oppressed, takes sides with black people. He is not color blind in the black-white struggle, but has made an unqualified identification with black people. This means that the movement for black liberation is the work of God himself, effecting his will among men.

Thirdly, there are, to be sure, many people who suffer, and they are not all black. Many white liberals receive a certain joy in reminding black militants that two thirds of the poor in America are white people. Of course one could observe that this means that the proportion of poor blacks is five times as great as that of poor whites, when we consider the total population of each group. But it is not our intention to debate white liberals on this issue, since it is not the purpose of Black Theology to minimize the suffering of others, including white people. Black Theology merely tries to discern the activity of the Holy One as he effects his purpose in the liberation of man from the forces of oppression. We *must* make decisions about where God is at work so we can join him in his fight against evil. But

there is no perfect guide for discerning God's movement in the world. Contrary to what many conservatives would say, the Bible is not a blueprint on this
matter. It is a valuable symbol for pointing to God's
revelation in Christ, but it is not self-interpreting. We
are thus placed in an existential situation of freedom in
which the burden is on us to make the decision without a guaranteed ethical guide. This is the risk of faith.
For the black theologian God is at work in the black
community, vindicating black people against white oppression. It is impossible for him to be indifferent on
this issue. Either God is for black people in their fight
for liberation and against the white oppressors, or he is
not. He cannot be both for us and for white oppressors at the same time.

In this connection we may observe that Black Theology takes seriously Paul Tillich's description of the
symbolic nature of all theological speech.[3] Man cannot
describe God directly; he must use symbols that point
to dimensions of reality that cannot be spoken of literally. Therefore to speak of Black Theology is to speak
with the Tillichian understanding of symbol in mind.
The focus on blackness does not mean that *only* blacks
suffer as victims in a racist society, but that blackness
is an ontological symbol and a visible reality which
best describes what oppression means in America. The
extermination of Indians, the persecution of the Jews,

[3] See Paul Tillich, *Dynamics of Faith* (New York: Harper and
Brothers, 1957).

the oppression of Mexican Americans, and every other conceivable inhumanity done in the name of God and country—these brutalities can be analyzed in terms of America's inability to recognize humanity in persons of color. If the oppressed of this land want to challenge the oppressive character of white society, they must begin by affirming their identity in terms of that reality which is antiwhite. Blackness, then, stands for all victims of oppression who realize that their humanity is inseparable from man's liberation from whiteness.[4]

[4] I do not intend to qualify this statement because too much is at stake—the survival of the black community. But perhaps some clarification is needed here. Some critics will undoubtedly ask, "How can you dismiss out of hand any criticisms that white theologians or others in traditional white Christianity might raise concerning your interpretation of Black Theology, and at the same time, use quotations from white theologians, both European and American, with approval? If white theology is as bad as you say, why not dismiss them altogether, without any reference to their work?" Of course, these are challenging questions, and I can see white people milking this idea for all that it's worth.

There are essentially two responses. First, those who press this point have taken too seriously the American definition of white. When I say that white theology is not Christian theology, I mean that theology which has been written without any reference to the oppressed of the land. This is not true of Karl Barth and certainly not true of Dietrich Bonhoeffer. Even Reinhold Niebuhr's *Moral Man and Immoral Society* moves in the direction of blackness. To decide the blackness of a particular perspective, we need only ask, "For whom was it written, the oppressed or the oppressors?" If the former, it is black; if the latter, it is white. I do not condemn all men who happen to look like white Americans; the condemnation comes when they act like them.

Secondly, it is characteristic of oppression to be limited to the thought forms of him who calls himself the master. Oppression refers not only to economic, social and political disfranchisement; there is the disfranchisement of the mind, the spiritual and moral values that hold together one's identity in a community. To be oppressed is to

With such a definition of blackness, we may see blackness as the most adequate symbol for pointing to the dimensions of divine activity in America. And insofar as this country is seeking to make whiteness the dominating power throughout the world, whiteness is the symbol for the Antichrist. Whiteness symbolizes the activity of deranged men intrigued by their own image of themselves, and thus unable to see that they are what is wrong with the world. Black Theology seeks to analyze the satanic nature of whiteness and by doing so to prepare all nonwhites for revolutionary action.

In passing, it may be worthwhile to point out that white people are in no position whatever to question the legitimacy of Black Theology. Questions like "Do you think theology is black?" or "What about others who suffer?" are the product of minds incapable of *black* thinking. It is not surprising that the people who reject blackness in theology are usually whites who do not question the blue-eyed white Christ. It is impos-

---

be defined, located or set aside according to another's perspective. This is precisely what has happened to the black person in America. If he would be free, he must use the thought forms of the master and transform them into ideas of liberation. If the black man were not enslaved but clearly understood the meaning of his spirituality from his own vantage point, he would not be oppressed. The task of Black Theology is to take Christian tradition that is so white and make it black, by showing that the white man does not know really what he is saying when he affirms Jesus as the Christ. He who has come to redeem us is not white but black; and the redemption of which he speaks has nothing to do with stabilizing the status quo. It motivates man to be what he is—a free creature.

[handwritten margin note: ...example of an intellectual point that does relate directly to real world - unlike so many intellectual points that don't make that connection with things people in the world care about -]

sible to believe that white people are worried about
Black Theology on account of its alleged alienation
of other sufferers. The oppressor is not genuinely concerned about *any* oppressed group. It would seem
rather that white rejection of Black Theology stems
from a recognition of the revolutionary implications in
the very phrase: a rejection of whiteness, an unwillingness to live under it, and an identification of
whiteness with evil and blackness with good.

Black Theology and the Black Community

Most theologians agree that theology is a church discipline, *i.e.*, a discipline which functions within the
Christian community. This is one aspect which distinguishes theology from philosophy of religion. Philosophy of religion is not committed to a community; but it
is an individual attempt to analyze the nature of ultimate reality through rational thought alone, using
elements of many different religions to assist in the articulation of the ultimate.

Theology by contrast cannot be separated from the
community which it represents. It assumes that *truth*
has been given in the moment of the community's
birth. Its task is to analyze the implications of that
truth, in order to make sure that the community remains committed to that which defines its existence.
Theology is the community's continued attempt to de-

fine in every generation its reason for being in the world. A community that does not analyze its existence theologically is a community that does not care what it says or does. It is a community which has no identity.

Applying this description, it is evident that white American theology has served the oppressors well. Throughout the history of this country, from the Puritans to the death-of-God theologians, the theological problems emanating from the white churches and theological schools are defined in such a manner that they are unrelated to the problem of being black in a white racist society. By defining the problems of Christianity independently of the black condition, white theology becomes a theology of white oppressors, serving as a divine sanction for criminal acts committed against black people. No white theologian has ever taken the oppression of black people as a point of departure for analyzing God's activity in contemporary America. Apparently white theologians see no connection between whiteness and evil or blackness and God. Even those white theologians who *try* to write books about black people invariably fail to. say anything relevant to the black community as it seeks to break the power of white racism. They usually think that writing books makes them experts on black humanity. As a result they are as arrogant as George Wallace in telling black people what is "best" for them. It is no surprise that the "best" is always the nonviolent way, the way least threatening to the political and social interests of the white majority.

Since white theology has consistently preserved the integrity of the community of oppressors, we conclude that it is not Christian theology at all.[5] When we speak about God as he is related to man in the black-white struggle, Christian theology can only mean Black Theology, a theology that speaks of God as he is related to black liberation. If we agree that the gospel of God is the proclamation of God's liberating activity, that the Christian community is an oppressed community that participates in that activity, and that theology is that discipline arising from within the Christian community as it seeks to develop adequate language for its relationship to God's liberation, then Black Theology is Christian theology.

It is unthinkable that the oppressors could identify with oppressed existence and thus say something relevant about God's liberation of the oppressed. In order to be Christian theology, white theology must cease being *white* theology and become Black Theology by denying whiteness as a proper form of human existence

[5] The reader should take note of the two characteristics of the definition of blackness. First, blackness is a *physiological* trait. It refers to a particular black-skinned people in America who have been victims of white racist brutality. These are the people who have the scars that bear witness to the inhumanity committed against them. Black Theology believes that they are the *only* key that can open the door to divine revelation. Therefore, no American theology can even tend in the direction of Christian theology without coming to terms with the black-skinned people of America. Secondly, blackness is an *ontological* symbol for all people who participate in the liberation of man from oppression. This is the universal note in Black Theology. It believes that all men were created for freedom, and that God always sides with the oppressed against the oppressors.

and affirming blackness as God's intention for humanity. White theologians will find this difficult, and it is to be expected that some will attempt to criticize Black Theology precisely at this point. Such criticism will not reveal the weakness in Black Theology but only the racist character of the critic.

Black Theology will not spend too much time trying to answer the critics because it is accountable only to the black community. Refusing to be separated from that community, Black Theology seeks to articulate the theological self-determination of black people, providing some ethical and religious categories for the black revolution in America. It says that all acts which participate in the destruction of white racism are Christian, the liberating deeds of God. All acts which impede the struggle of black self-determination—Black Power—are anti-Christian, the work of Satan.

The revolutionary situation forces Black Theology to shun all abstract principles dealing with what is the "right" and "wrong" course of action. There is only one principle which guides the thinking and action of Black Theology: an unqualified commitment to the black community as that community seeks to define its existence in the light of God's liberating work in the world. This means that Black Theology refuses to be guided by ideas and concepts alien to black people. It assumes that whites encountering black thought will judge it "irrational." Not understanding the oppressed condition, the oppressor is in no position to understand the methods which the oppressed use in liberation. The logic of liberation is always incomprehensible to the slave masters. In the position of power, masters never understand what the slaves mean by "dignity." The only dignity they know is that of killing the slaves, as if their humanity depends on the enslavement of others. Black Theology does not intend to debate with whites who have this perspective. Speaking for the black community, Black Theology says with Eldridge Cleaver, "We shall have our manhood. We shall have it, or the earth will be leveled by our attempts to gain it."

Black Theology as Survival Theology

To speak of Black Theology as survival theology refers to the *condition* of the community out of which Black Theology arises. We can delineate three characteristics of the black condition: the tension between life and death, identity crisis, and white social and political power.

1. *The Tension between Life and Death.* Black Theology is a theology of a community whose daily energies must be focused on physical survival in a hostile environment. The black community spends most of its time trying "to make a living" in a society labeled "for white only." Therefore, the central question for black people is "How are we going to survive in a world which deems black humanity as an illegitimate form of

human existence?" That white America has issued the
death warrant for being black is evident in the white
brutality inflicted on black people. Though whites may
pretend that it is not so, the present ghettos of this
country say otherwise. The masters always pretend
that they are not masters, insisting that they are only
doing what is best for the society as a whole, including
the slaves. This is, of course, the standard rhetoric of
an oppressive society. The blacks know better. They
know that whites have only one purpose: the destruction of everything which is not white. In this situation,
blacks are constantly asking, often unconsciously,
"When will the white overlord decide that blackness in
any form must be exterminated?" The genocide of the
American Indian is a reminder to the black community
that white people are capable of pursuing a course of
complete annihilation of everything black. And the
killing and the caging of black leaders make us think
that black genocide has already begun. It seems that,
from the white cop on his beat to the high government
official, white people are not prepared for a real encounter with black reality, and thus the black community knows that whites may decide at any moment that
the entire extermination of all blacks is indispensable
to their existence as white people.

This is the content of "the tension between life and
death." By white definitions whiteness is "being" and
blackness is "nonbeing." For black people to affirm
their being in this situation is to live under sentence of

death. They know that whites will kill them rather than to permit the beauty and the glory of black humanity to be manifested in its fullness. Over 350 years of black slavery is evidence of that fact, and blacks must carve out an existence in this situation. To breathe in white society is dependent on saying Yes to whiteness, and black people know it.

It is only natural for one to cling to life, for no one wants to die. But there is such a thing as living physically while being dead spiritually. As long as blacks let white define the limits of their being, black people are dead. "To be, or not to be" is thus a dilemma for the black community: to assert one's humanity and be killed, or to cling to life and sink into nonhumanity.

It is in this situation that Black Theology seeks to speak the Word of God. It says that the God who revealed himself in the life of oppressed Israel and who came to us in the Incarnate Christ and is present today as Holy Spirit has made a decision about the black condition. He has chosen to make the black condition his condition! It is a continuation of his incarnation in twentieth-century America. This means that God has taken sides in this struggle; and his righteousness will liberate the oppressed of this nation and "all flesh shall see it together." It is this certainty that makes physical life less than ultimate and thus enables black people courageously to affirm blackness and its liberating power as ultimate. When people feel this way, a revolution is in the making. With the assurance that God is on our side, we can begin to make ready for the inevitable—the decisive encounter between black and white existence. White appeals to "wait and talk it over" are irrelevant when children are dying and men and women are being tortured. We will not let whitey cool this one with his pious love ethic but will seek to enhance our hostility, bringing it to its full manifestation. Black survival is at stake here, and we black people must define and assert the conditions necessary for our being-in-the-world. Only we can decide how much we can endure from the white racists. And as we make our decision in the midst of life and death, being and nonbeing, the role of Black Theology is to articulate this decision by pointing to the revelation of God in the black liberation struggle.

2. *Identity Crisis.* There is more at stake in the struggle for survival than mere physical existence. You have to be *black* with a knowledge of the history of this country to know what America means to black people. You also have to know what it means to be a nonperson, a nothing, a person with no past to know what Black Power is all about. Survival as a person means not only food and shelter, but also belonging to a community that remembers and understands the meaning of its past. Black consciousness is an attempt to recover a past deliberately destroyed by slave masters, an attempt to revive old survival symbols and create new ones.

"History's potency is mighty," writes Herbert Aptheker. "The oppressed need it for identity and inspiration; oppressors for justification, rationalization and legitimacy. Nothing illustrates this more clearly than the history writing on the American Negro people." [6] White Americans must convince themselves that they have been innocent in view of the historical circumstances, but black people have a different way of evaluating the history of this country. For them Americans have pursued two principal courses in regard to black people. First, this country legally defined black people outside the realm of humanity, decreeing that blacks were animals and that their own enslavement was best both for them and the society as a whole. And as long as black labor was needed, slavery was always regarded as the only appropriate solution to the "black problem." But when black labor was no longer needed, the blacks were issued their "freedom," the freedom to live in a society which attempted to destroy them physically and spiritually. There is no indication before or after the Civil War that this society recognized the humanity of black people.

The second course of action which whites have taken is to try to "integrate" blacks into white society. Before the Supreme Court decision in 1954, whites sought to destroy black identity by segregating blacks from the mainstream of the society, thus declaring that this world is not for black people. Then under the ban-

[6] Quoted in J. H. Clarke, ed., *William Styron's Nat Turner: Ten Black Writers Respond* (Boston: Beacon Press, 1968), p. vii.

ner of liberalism (compounded of white guilt and black naïveté), "integration" became the watchword. The implications of the term are now all too clear: the destruction of black identity through assimilation. They want to integrate us black people into *their* society—straight hair, neckties, deodorant, the whole package—as if we had no existence apart from whiteness.

In a situation like this, there is only one course of action for the black community, and that is to destroy the oppressor's definition of blackness by unraveling new meanings in old tales so that the past may emerge as an instrument of black liberation. If the oppressed are to preserve their personhood, they must create a new way of looking at history independent of the perspective of the oppressor. Black Theology is survival theology because it seeks to provide the theological dimensions of the struggle for black identity. It seeks to reorder religious language, to show that all forces supporting white oppression are anti-Christian in their essence. The essence of the gospel of Christ stands or falls on the question of black humanity, and there is no way that a church or institution can be related to the gospel of Christ if it sponsors or tolerates racism in any form. To speak of a "racist Christian" or a "segregated church of Christ" is blasphemy and thus has nothing whatsoever to do with the Christian gospel.

In another connection, Paul Tillich wrote: "Man discovers himself when he discovers God; he discovers something that is identical with himself although it transcends him infinitely, something from which he is estranged, but from which he never has been and never can be separated." [7] Despite the pantheistic implications, there is some truth implied here which is applicable to the black identity crisis. The search for black identity is the search for God, for God's identity is black identity. For Black Theology, this is not pantheism; it is the conviction that the transcendent God who became immanent in Israelite history and incarnate in the man Jesus is also involved in the history of black people, effecting their liberation from white oppressors. This is what Black Theology means for black people who are in search of new ways of talking about God which enhances their understanding of themselves.

3. *White Social and Political Power*. Black Theology is the theological expression of a people who lack social and political power. Despite the economic plight of whites, they can manage to transcend the oppression of the society, but there is nothing blacks can do to escape the humiliation of white supremacy except to affirm the very attribute which the oppressors find unacceptable. It is clear to black people why they are unwanted in the society, and for years they tried to make themselves acceptable in spite of their blackness by playing the game of human existence according to

[7] Tillich, *The Theology of Culture* (New York: Oxford University Press, 1959), p. 10.

white rules, hoping that some day white people would not regard the color of their skins as the criterion for human relationships. But to this day, there is little evidence that whites can deal with the reality of physical blackness as an appropriate form of human existence. For this reason, black people are oppressed socially even if they have economic and intellectual power. In Nazi Germany, the Jews found out the hard way that there was no security in economic power against an insane people who had the political and social power to determine Jewish existence. Realizing that white racism is an insanity comparable to Nazism, Black Theology seeks to articulate a theological ethos that is consistent with the black revolutionary struggle. Black people know that there is only one possible authentic existence in this society, and that is to force a radical revolutionary confrontation with the structures of white power by saying Yes to the essence of their black being. The role of Black Theology is to tell black people to focus on their own self-determination as a community by preparing to do anything which the community believes to be necessary for its existence.

To be human in a condition of social oppression always involves affirming that which the oppressor regards as degrading. In a world in which the oppressor defines right in terms of whiteness, humanity means an unqualified identification with blackness. Black, therefore, is beautiful because the oppressor has made it ugly. We glorify it because they despise it; we love it because

they hate it. It is the black way of saying, "To hell with
your stinking white society and its middle class ideas
about the world. I will have no part in it."

The white view of black humanity also has *political*
ramifications. That is why so much emphasis has been
placed on "law and order" recently. Black people live
in a society in which blackness means criminality, and
thus "law and order" means "get blacky." To live, to
stay out of jail, blacks are required to obey laws of humiliation. "Law and order" is nothing but an emphasis
on the stabilization of the *status quo,* which means telling blacks they cannot be black and telling whites that
they have the moral and political right to see to it that
black people stay in their "place." Conversely the development of Black Power means that the black community will define its own place, its own way of behav-
ing in the world, regardless of the consequences to
white society. We have reached our limit of tolerance,
and if it means death with dignity, or life with humiliation, we will choose the former. And if that is the
choice, we will take some honkies with us. What is to
be hoped is that there can be a measure of existence in
dignity in this society for black people so that we do
not have to *prove* that we have reached the limits of
suffering. But the man in political power is a strange
creature, and it is very easy for him to believe that
human dignity has no real meaning. In André Malraux's *Man's Fate,* Konig, chief of Chiang Kai-shek's
police, illustrates the inability of the man in political
power to understand the condition of the oppressed.

Intrigued by Kyo's participation in the Shanghai insurrection, Konig asks his prisoner, "I have been told that you are a communist through dignity. Is that true?" Kyo replies: "I think that communism will make dignity possible for those with whom I am fighting."

But Konig asks, "What do you call dignity? It doesn't mean anything." "The opposite of humiliation," says Kyo. "When one comes from where I come, that means something." [8] But since oppressors do not come from the land of the oppressed, they do not have to attach any meaning to the demands of the oppressed.

We can conclude then that the element of survival is a way of living for the black community. Black Theology is a theology of survival because it seeks to interpret the theological significance of the being of a community whose existence is threatened by the power of nonbeing. We are seeking meaning in a world permeated with philosophical and theological absurdities, where hope is nonexistent. In existential philosophy the absurd is "that which is meaningless."

> Thus man's existence is absurd because his contingency finds no external justification. His projects are absurd because they are directed toward an unattainable goal.[9]

This is certainly the feeling of black people as they seek to make sense out of their existence in a white so-

[8] André Malraux, *Man's Fate*, trans. by Hookon Chevalier (New York: Modern Library, 1961), p. 306.

[9] Jean-Paul Sartre, *Being and Nothingness*, trans. by Hazel Barnes (New York: Philosophical Library, 1956), p. 628.

ciety. What can we say to a community whose suffering and humiliation is beyond any rational explication? The black condition is inflicted by the white condition and there is no rational explanation of it.

Speaking to the black condition characterized by existential absurdities, Black Theology rejects the tendency of classical Christianity to appeal to divine providence. To suggest that black suffering is consistent with the knowledge and will of God and that in the end everything will happen for the good of those who love God is unacceptable to black people. The eschatological promise of heaven is insufficient to account for the earthly pain of black suffering. We cannot accept a God who inflicts or tolerates black suffering for some inscrutable purpose.

Black Theology also rejects those who counsel black people to accept the limits which this society places on them, since that is tantamount to suicide. In existential philosophy suicide is the ultimate expression of despair. If we accept white definitions of blackness, we destroy ourselves.

Black Theology, responding to the black condition, takes on the character of rebellion against things as they are. In Camus's writings, the rebel is the man who refuses to accept the absurd conditions of things but fights against them in spite of the impossibility of arriving at a solution. In Black Theology, black people are encouraged to revolt against the structures of white social and political power by affirming blackness, not be-

←) this is answer to objection - in a
theology that identifies God w/ oppressed,
what if no oppressed ? -
- will always be oppressed

cause blacks have a chance of "winning." What could
the concept of "winning" possibly mean? Black people
do what they do because and only because they can do
no other; and Black Theology says simply that such action is in harmony with the revealed activity of God.

Black Theology as Passionate Language

Because Black Theology is survival theology, it must
speak with a passion consistent with the depths of the
wounds of the oppressed. Theological language is passionate language, the language of commitment, because it is language which seeks to vindicate the afflicted and condemn the enforcers of evil. Christian
theology cannot afford to be an abstract, dispassionate
discourse on the nature of God in relation to man, as if
such an analysis has no ethical implications for the contemporary forms of oppression in our society. Theology
must take the risk of faith, knowing that it stands on
the edge of condemnation by the forces of evil. Paul
Tillich calls this an "existential risk." "The risk of faith
is an existential risk, a risk in which the meaning and
fulfillment of our lives is at stake, and not a theoretical
judgment which may be refuted sooner or later." [10]
Black people know what it means to have their lives at
stake, for their lives are at stake every moment of their
existence. In the black world this is no time to take life

[10] Tillich, *op. cit.*, p. 28.

for granted, since every moment of being is surrounded with the threat of nonbeing. And if Black Theology is to relate itself to this situation, it too must take the risk of faith and speak with a passion which is in harmony with the revolutionary spirit of the oppressed.

The sin of American theology is that it has spoken without passion. It has failed miserably in relating its work to the oppressed in society by refusing to confront the structures of this nation with the evils of racism. When it has tried to speak for the poor, it has been so cool and calm in its analysis of human evil that it implicitly disclosed whose side it was on. Most of the time American theology has simply remained silent, ignoring the condition of the victims of this racist society. How else can we explain the theological silence during the period of white lynching of black humanity in this nation? How else can we explain the inability of white religionists to deal relevantly with the new phenomenon of black consciousness? And how else can we explain the problem white seminaries are having as they seek to respond to radical black demands? There is really only one answer: American theology is racist; it identifies theology as dispassionate analysis of "the tradition," unrelated to the sufferings of the oppressed.

Black Theology rejects this approach and views theology as a participation in passion on behalf of the oppressed. Seeking to be Christian theology in an age of societal dehumanization, it contemplates the ultimate possibility of nonbeing (death) with the full intention of affirming the ultimate possibility of being (life). In the struggle for truth in a revolutionary age, there can be no principles of truth, no absolutes, not even God. For we realize that, though the reality of God must be the presupposition of theology (the very name implies this—*theos* and *logos*), we cannot speak of him at the expense of the oppressed.

The insistence on a passionate theology is a call for an anthropocentric point of departure in theology. We realize that such a call must raise the eyebrows of all who have felt the impact of Karl Barth. But let us state clearly that this approach is not a return to nineteenth-century liberalism with its emphasis on the goodness and worth of man (which always meant white European man). Every black intellectual is aware that when liberals spoke of inevitable progress and the upward movement of Western culture, they did so at the expense of black men who were enslaved and colonized to secure "progress." Our concern is altogether different. Though our perspective begins with man, it is not man in general, not some abstract species of Platonic idealism. We are concerned with concrete man, particularly with oppressed man. In America that means the black man. This is the point of departure of Black Theology, because it believes that oppressed man is the point of departure of Christ himself. It is this concern that makes theological language a language of passion.

Our definition of Black Theology as passionate theology is analogous to Paul Tillich's analysis of "the Existential thinker." Quoting Feuerbach, he writes:

> Do not wish to be a philosopher in contrast to being a man . . . do not think as a thinker . . . think as a living, real being . . . think in Existence. Love is passion, and only passion is the mark of Existence.[11]

In fact, Tillich quotes Feuerbach as saying, "Only what is as an object of passion—really is." [12] The existential thinker is a thinker who not only relates thought to existence but whose thought arises out of a passionate encounter with existence. As Kierkegaard put it in his definition of truth: "An objective uncertainty held fast in the most passionate personal experience is the truth, the highest truth attainable for an Existing individual." [13] Relating this to Black Theology, we can say that the definition of truth for the black thinker arises from a passionate encounter with black reality. Though that truth may be described religiously as God, it is not the God of white religion but the God of black existence. There is no way to speak of this objectively; truth is not objective. It is subjective, a personal experience of the ultimate in the midst of degradation. Passion is the only appropriate response to this truth.

To be passionate theology, Black Theology may find it necessary to break with the traditional theological concerns. Such concerns are often unrelated to op-

[11] Tillich, *op. cit.*, pp. 89-90.
[12] *Ibid.*, p. 90.
[13] Quoted in *ibid.*, p. 90.

pressed existence. Like the pre-Civil war black preachers, it believes that racism is incompatible with the gospel of Christ, and it must, therefore, do everything it can to reveal the satanic nature of racism, so that it can be destroyed. It will be difficult for white theologians to participate in this reality because of their identification with unreality. Creative theological reflection about God and his movement in the world is possible only when one frees himself from the powers that be. The mind must be freed from the values of the oppressive society. It involves prophetic condemnation of the society so that God's Word can be clearly distinguished from the words of men. Such a task is especially difficult in America, a nation demonically deceived about what is good, true, and beautiful. The oppression in this country is sufficiently camouflaged so that it is possible to believe that things are not really too bad. White theologians, not having felt the sting of oppression, will find it most difficult to criticize this nation for the condemnation of America means a condemnation of self.

The true black thinker is in a different position. He cannot be *black* and be identified with the powers that be. To be black is to be committed to destroying everything this country loves and adores. Creativity and passion are possible when one stands where the black man stands, a creature who has visions of the future because the present is unbearable. And the black man will cling to that future as a means of passionately rejecting the present.

II

The Sources
and Norm
of Black Theology

The Function of the Sources and Norm

Though I have alluded already to some of the factors which shape the perspective of Black Theology, it is necessary to say a word about what are often designated as sources and norm in systematic theology. The sources are the "formative factors" [1] that determine the character of a given theology, and the norm is "the criterion to which the sources . . . must be subjected." [2]

---

[1] See John Macquarrie, *Principles of Christian Theology* (New York: Charles Scribner's Sons, 1966), p. 4.

[2] Tillich, *Systematic Theology*, Vol. I (Chicago: The University of Chicago Press, 1951), p. 47.

That is, the sources are the relevant data for the theological task, while the norm determines how the data will be used. It is often the case that different theologies share the same sources, and it is the theological norm which elevates one particular source (or sources) to a dominating role.

Karl Barth and Paul Tillich provide useful examples. Both agree that the Bible and culture are important data for the theological discipline. But an examination of each man's work shows that culture plays a much larger role in Tillich's theology, while the Bible is crucial for Barth. For Barth Scripture is the witness to the Word of God and thus is indispensable to doing theology. Tillich, on the other hand, agrees that the Bible is important, but holds that the task of making the gospel relevant to contemporary man is equally important. If pressed, Barth (at least in his later years) would not deny that Tillich's concern for relevance is a legitimate concern; yet Barth is skeptical about regarding culture as a point of departure for theology. God is still God and man is man, even for the later Barth. That being the case, the only legitimate starting point of theology is the man Jesus who is the revelation of God. Whatever is said about culture must be said in the light of this prior perspective. But this style of theology worries Tillich. He wonders whether kerygmatic theologians like Barth are giving answers to questions that modern man is not asking. Culture—that is, the situation of modern man—must be the point of departure of relevant theology. For Tillich the danger of confusing the divine and the human, which is so important for Barth, is not nearly so important as the danger of giving answers that are irrelevant. In fact, the divine-human identity is the risk of faith. "The risk of faith is based on the fact that the unconditional element can become a matter of ultimate concern only if it appears in a concrete embodiment." [3] It is the "concrete embodiment" of the infinite which must be taken seriously. Culture then is the medium through which man encounters the divine and thus makes a decision.

Barth and Tillich illustrate the role that sources and norm play in shaping the character of a theology. Though their sources are similar, they do not agree on the norm. It is clear in Tillich's writings that the apologetic situation is decisive in defining the norm of systematic theology; and he identifies the norm as "New Being in Jesus as the Christ" which is the only answer to man's estrangement. While Tillich appeals to the cultural situation regarding the norm, Barth is kerygmatic in that he defines the man Jesus as witnessed to in the Holy Scriptures as the only norm for God-talk.

It is clear, therefore, that the most important decisions in theology are made at this juncture. The sources and norm are presuppositions that determine which questions are to be asked, as well as the answers that are given. Believing that the biblical Christ is the sole criterion for theology, Barth not only asks ques-

[3] Tillich, *Theology of Culture*, p. 28.

tions about man that arise from a study of Christology, but he also derives his answers from the man Jesus. Tillich, on the other hand, deals with questions that arise from the cultural situation of man, and endeavors to shape his answers according to that situation. Both approaches are conditioned by their theological perspectives.

Because a perspective refers to the whole of a man's being in the context of a community, the sources and norm of Black Theology must be consistent with the perspective of the black community. Since white American theologians do not belong to the black community, they cannot relate the gospel to that community. Invariably, when white theology attempts to speak to the black people about Jesus Christ, the gospel is presented in the light of the social, political, and economic interest of the white majority. (One example of this is the interpretation of Christian love as nonviolence.) Black theologians must work in such a way as to destroy the corruptive influence of white thought by building theology on the sources and norm that are appropriate to the black community.

The Sources of Black Theology

There are many factors which shape the perspective of Black Theology. Since black consciousness is a relatively new phenomenon, it is too early to define all of the sources which are participating in its creation. The black community as a self-determining people, proud of its blackness, has just begun, and we must wait before we can describe what its fullest manifestation will be. "We are God's children now; it does not yet appear what we shall be . . ." (I John 3:2a). Even so, at this stage, we must say a word about the present manifestation. What are the sources in Black Theology?

1. Black Experience. There can be no Black Theology which does not take seriously the black experience —a life of humiliation and suffering. This must be the point of departure of all God-talk which seeks to be black-talk. This means that Black Theology realizes that it is man who speaks of God; and when that man is black, he can only speak of God in the light of the black experience. It is not that Black Theology denies the importance of God's revelation in Christ; but black people want to know what Christ means when they are confronted with the brutality of white racism. The black experience prevents us from turning the gospel into theological catch phrases and makes us realize that they must be clothed in black flesh. The black experience forces us to ask, "What does revelation mean when one's being is engulfed in a system of white racism cloaking itself in pious moralities?" "What does God mean when a policeman whacks you over the head because you are black?" "What does the Church mean when white churchmen proclaim they need more time to end racism?"

The black experience should not be identified with inwardness, as implied in Schleiermacher's description of religion as the "feeling of absolute dependence." It is not an introspection in which man contemplates his own ego. Black people are not afforded the luxury of navel gazing. The black experience is the environment in which black people live. It is the totality of black existence in a white world where babies are tortured, women are raped, and men are shot. The black poet Don Lee puts it well: "The true black experience in most cases is very concrete . . . sleeping in subways, being bitten by rats, six people living in a kitchenette." [4]

The black experience is existence in a system of white racism. The black man knows that a ghetto is the white way of saying that black people are subhuman and fit only to live with rats. The black experience is police departments recruiting more men and buying more guns to provide "law and order," which means making the city safe for white people. It is politicians telling blacks to cool it *or else*. It is George Wallace, Hubert Humphrey, and Richard Nixon running for President and Nixon winning. The black experience is college administrators defining "quality" education in the light of white values. It is church bodies compromising and debating whether blacks are human. And because Black Theology is a product of that experience, it must talk about God

[4] David Llorens, "Black Don Lee," *Ebony*, March 1969, p. 74.

in the light of it. The purpose of Black Theology is to make sense of black experience.

The black experience, however, is more than encountering white insanity. It also means black people making decisions about themselves which involve white people. Black people know that white people do not have the last word on black existence. This realization may be defined as Black Power, which is the power of the black community to make decisions regarding its identity. When this happens, black people become aware of their blackness; and to be aware of self is to set certain limits on other people's behavior toward oneself. The black experience means telling whitey what the limits are.

The power of the black experience cannot be overestimated. It is the power to love oneself precisely because one is black and a readiness to die if white people try to make one behave otherwise. It is the sound of James Brown singing, "I'm Black and I'm Proud" and Aretha Franklin demanding "Respect." The black experience is catching the spirit of blackness and loving it. It is hearing black preachers speak of God's love in spite of the filthy ghetto, and black congregations responding, "Amen," which means that they realize that ghetto-existence is not the result of divine decree but of white inhumanity. The black experience is the feeling one has when he strikes against the enemy of black humanity by throwing a live Molotov cocktail into a white-owned building and watching it go up in flames. We know, of course, that there is more to getting rid of evil than burning buildings, but one must start somewhere.

Being black is a beautiful experience. It is the sane way of living in an insane environment. Whites do not understand it; they can only catch glimpses of it in sociological reports and historical studies. The black experience is possible only for black people. It means having natural hair cuts, wearing African dashikis and dancing to the sound of Johnny Lee Hooker or B. B. King, knowing that no matter how hard whitey tries, there can be no real duplication of black soul. Black soul is not learned; it comes from the totality of black experience, the experience of carving out an existence in a society that says you don't belong.

The black experience is a source of Black Theology because the latter seeks to relate biblical revelation to the situation of black people in America. This means that Black Theology cannot speak of God and his activity in contemporary America without identifying him with the liberation of the black community.

2. *Black History*. Black history refers to the way black people were brought to this land and the way they have been treated in this land. This is not to say that only the American white man participated in the institution of slavery. But there was something unique about American slavery, namely, the white man's attempt to define black people as nonpeople. In other countries the slaves were allowed community, and

there were slave rights. Slaves were human beings, and their humanity was protected (to some degree) by certain civil laws. Black history in America means that white people used every conceivable method to destroy black humanity. As late as 1857 the highest court of this land decreed that black people "had no rights which the white man was bound to respect." The history of slavery in this country reveals the possibilities of human depravity; and the fact that this country still, in many blatant ways, perpetuates the idea of the inferiority of black people shows the capabilities of human evil. If Black Theology is going to speak to the condition of black people, it cannot ignore the history of white inhumanity committed against them.

But black history is more than what whites did to blacks. More importantly black history is black people saying No to every act of white brutality. Contrary to what whites say in *their* history books, Black Power is not new. It began when the first black man decided that he had had enough of white domination. It began when black mothers decided to kill their babies rather than have them grow up to be slaves. Black Power is Nat Turner, Denmark Vesey, and Gabriel Prosser planning a slave revolt. It is slaves poisoning masters, and Frederick Douglass delivering an abolitionist address. This is the history that Black Theology must take seriously before it can begin to speak about God and black people.

Like Black Power, Black Theology is not new either.

It came into being when black churchmen realized that killing slave masters was doing the work of God. It began when black churchmen refused to accept the racist white church as consistent with the gospel of God. The organizing of the African Methodist Episcopal Church, The African Methodist Episcopal Zion Church, the Christian Methodist Church, the Baptist Churches and many other black churches is a visible manifestation of Black Theology. The participation of the black churches in the black liberation struggle from the eighteenth to the twentieth century is a tribute to the endurance of Black Theology.

Black Theology focuses on black history as a source for its theological interpretation of God's work in the world because divine activity is inseparable from the history of black people. There can be no comprehension of Black Theology without realizing that its existence comes from a community which looks back on its unique past, visualizes the reality of the future, and then makes decisions about possibilities in the present. Taking seriously the reality of God's involvement in history, Black Theology asks, "What are the implications of black history for the revelation of God? Is he active in black history or has he withdrawn and left black people at the disposal of white insanity?" While the answers to these questions are not easy, Black Theology refuses to accept a God who is not identified totally with the goals of the black community. If God is not for us and against white people, then he is a murderer, and we had better kill him. The task of Black Theology is to kill gods who do not belong to the black community; and by taking black history as a source, we know that this is neither an easy nor a sentimental task but an awesome responsibility.

3. *Black Culture.* The concept of black culture is closely related to black experience and black history. We could say that the black experience is what the black man feels when he tries to carve out an existence in dehumanized white society. It is black "soul," the pain and the joy of reacting to whiteness and affirming blackness. Black history is the record of the joy and the pain. It is those experiences that the black community remembers and retells because of the mythic power inherent in the symbols for the present revolution against white racism. Black culture consists of the creative forms of expression as one reflects on the history, endures the pain, and experiences the joy. It is the black community expressing itself in music, poetry, prose and other art forms. The emergence of the concept of the Revolutionary Black Theatre with writers like LeRoi Jones, Larry Neal, Ed Bullins, and others is an example of the black community expressing itself culturally. Aretha Franklin, James Brown, Charlie Parker, John Coltrane, and others are examples in music. Culture refers to the way a man lives and moves in the world; it controls his thought forms.

Black Theology must take seriously the cultural expressions of the community it represents so that it will be able to speak relevantly to the black condition. Of course, Black Theology is aware of the danger of identifying the word of man with the Word of God, the danger Karl Barth persuasively warned against in the second decade of this century. "Form," he writes, "believes itself capable of taking the place of content. . . . Man has taken the divine in his possession; he has brought him under his management." [5] Such a warning is necessary in a situation alive with satanic creatures like Hitler, and it is always the task of the church to announce the impending judgment of God against the power of the state which seeks to destroy the weak. This is why Bonhoeffer said, "When Christ calls a man, he bids him come and die." Suffering is the badge of true discipleship. But is it appropriate to speak the same words to the oppressed? To apply Barth's words to the black-white context and interpret them as a warning against identifying God's revelation with black culture is to misunderstand Barth. His warning was appropriate for the situation in which it was given, but not for black people. Black people need to see some correlations between divine salvation and black culture. For too long Christ has been pictured as a blue-eyed honky. Black theologians are right: we need to dehonkify him and thus make him relevant to the black condition.

Paul Tillich wrote:

[5] Karl Barth, *The Word of God and the Word of Man*, trans. by Douglas Horton (New York: Harper and Row, Publishers, 1957), p. 68.

I am not unaware of the danger that in this way [the method of relating theology to culture] the substance of the Christian message may be lost. Nevertheless, this danger must be risked, and once one has realized this, one must proceed in this direction. Dangers are not a reason for avoiding a serious demand.[6]

Though Tillich was not speaking of the black situation, his words are applicable to it. To be sure, as Barth pointed out, God's Word is alien to man and thus comes to him as a "bolt from the blue," but one must be careful about which man one is speaking of. For the oppressors, the dehumanizers, the analysis is correct. However, when we speak of God's revelation to the oppressed, the analysis is incorrect. His revelation comes to us in and through the cultural situation of the oppressed. His Word is our word; his existence, our existence. This is the meaning of black culture and its relation to divine revelation.

Black culture, then, is God's way of acting in America, his participation in black liberation. Speaking of black art, Don Lee writes: "Black art will elevate and enlighten our people and lead them toward an awareness of self, *i.e.*, their blackness. It will show them mirrors. Beautiful symbols. And will aid in the destruction of anything nasty and detrimental to our advancement as a people." [7] This is black liberation, the emancipation of the minds and souls of black peo-

[6] Tillich, *Systematic Theology*, Vol. III, p. 4.
[7] Llorens, *op. cit.*, p. 73.

ple from white definitions of black humanity. Black Theology does not ignore this; it participates in this experience of the divine.

4. Revelation. Some religionists who have been influenced by the twentieth-century Protestant theologies of revelation will question my discussion of revelation as the fourth source rather than the *first*. Does this not suggest that revelation is secondary to the black experience, black history and black culture? Is not this the very danger which Karl Barth pointed to?

I should indicate that the numerical order of the discussion is not necessarily in order of importance. It is difficult to know which source is more important since all are interdependent and thus a discussion of one usually involves the others. No hard-and-fast line can be drawn between them. A perspective is an expression of the way a community perceives itself and its participation in reality, and this is a *total* experience. It is not possible to slice up that experience and rate the pieces in terms of importance. Since *being* refers to the whole of reality, talk about one aspect of being forces one to consider the totality of being. I have tried to choose a method of discussion which best describes the black community's encounter with reality.

I do not think that revelation is comprehensible from a black theological perspective without a prior understanding of the concrete manifestation of revelation in the black community as seen in the black experience, black history, and black culture. For Christian faith revelation is an event, a happening in human history. It is God making himself known to man through a historical act of human liberation. Revelation is what Yahweh *did* in the event of the Exodus; it is Yahweh tearing down old orders and establishing new ones. Throughout the entire history of Israel, to know God is to know what he is doing in human history on behalf of the oppressed of the land.

In the New Testament, the revelatory event of God takes place in the person of Christ. He is the event of God, telling us who God is by what he does on behalf of the oppressed. For Christian thinking the man Jesus must be the decisive interpretive factor in everything we say about God because he is the complete revelation of God.

This analysis of the meaning of revelation is not new in Protestant circles since the appearance of Karl Barth. The weakness of white American theology is that it seldom gets beyond the first century in its analysis of revelation. If I read the New Testament correctly, the resurrection of Christ means that he is also present today in the midst of all societies effecting his liberation of the oppressed. He is not confined to the first century, and thus our talk of him in the past is important only insofar as it leads us to an *encounter* with him *now*. As a black theologian, I want to know what God's revelation means right now as the black community participates in the struggle for liberation.

The failure of white theology to speak to the black liberation struggle only reveals once again the racist character of white thought.

For Black Theology, revelation is not *just* a past event or a contemporary event in which it is difficult to recognize the activity of God. *Revelation is a black event,* i.e., what black people are doing about their liberation. I have spoken of the black experience, black history, and black culture as theological sources because they are God himself at work liberating his people.

I am aware of a possible pantheistic distortion of my analysis. But this risk must be taken if theological statements are going to have meaning in a world that is falling apart because white people think that God has appointed them to rule over other people, especially black people. Besides, people who are unduly nervous about pantheism inevitably move toward a deistic distortion of faith; and the god of deism may as well be dead. Our risk is no greater than the risk inherent in Hebrew prophecy; and do I need to mention the risk of Christ? Christian theology, if it is going to have relevance in a revolutionary situation, must take the risk of pointing to the contemporary manifestation of God, and this necessarily involves taking sides. Should God's work in the world be identified with the oppressors or the oppressed? There can be no neutrality on this issue; neutrality is nothing but an identification of God's work with the oppressors.

Black Theology takes the risk of faith and thus makes an unqualified identification of God's revelation with the liberation of black people. There can be no other medium of encountering the contemporary revelatory event of God in this society.

5. *Scripture*. Black Theology is kerygmatic theology. That is, it is theology which takes seriously the importance of Scripture in theological discourse. There can be no theology of the Christian gospel which does not take into account the biblical witness. It is true that the Bible is not the revelation of God; only Christ is. But it is an indispensable witness to God's revelation and is thus a primary source for Christian thinking about God. As John Macquarrie says, "It is one important way . . . by which the community of faith keeps open its access to that primordial revelation on which the community has been founded." [8] By taking seriously the witness of Scripture, we are prevented from making the gospel into private moments of religious ecstasy or into the religious sanctification of the structures of society. The Bible can serve as a guide for checking the contemporary interpretation of God's revelation, making certain that our interpretation is consistent with the biblical witness.

It is indeed the *biblical* witness that says that God is a God of liberation, who calls to himself the oppressed and abused in the nation and assures them that his righteousness will vindicate their suffering. It is the

[8] Macquarrie, *op. cit.*, p. 8.

Bible that tells us that God became man in Jesus Christ so that his kingdom would make freedom a reality for all men. This is the meaning of the resurrection of Christ. Man no longer has to be a slave to anybody but must rebel against all the principalities and powers which make his existence subhuman. It is in this light that Black Theology is affirmed as a twentieth-century analysis of God's work in the world.

From this, however, we should not conclude that the Bible is an infallible witness. God is neither the author of the Bible, nor are the writers his secretaries. Efforts to prove verbal inspiration of the Scripture are the result of men failing to see the real meaning of the biblical message: the liberation of man! Unfortunately, it is the very emphasis on verbal infallibility which leads us to unimportant concerns. While churches are debating whether the whale swallowed Jonah, the state is enacting laws of inhumanity against the oppressed. It matters little to the oppressed who authored Scripture; what is important is whether it can serve as a weapon against the oppressors.

It is interesting that there is a close correlation between political and religious conservatism. Whites who insist on verbal infallibility are often the most violent racists. If one can be sure, without the possibility of doubt, regarding his view of Scripture, then he can be equally sure in enforcing his view in the society as a whole. With God on his side there is nothing that will be spared in the name of "the laws of God and men." It

becomes an easy matter to kill blacks, Indians, or anybody else who questions his right to make decisions on
how the world ought to be governed. Literalism always
means the removal of doubt in religion, and thus enables the believer to justify all kinds of political oppression in the name of God and country. During slavery
black people were encouraged to be obedient slaves
because it was the will of God. After all, Paul did say
"slaves obey your masters"; and because of the "curse
of Ham," blacks have been condemned to be inferior to
whites. Even today the same kind of literalism is being
used by white scholars to encourage black people to be
nonviolent, as if nonviolence were the only possible
expression of Christian love. It is surprising that it
never dawns on these white religionists that oppressors
are in no moral position to dictate what a Christian response is. Jesus' exhortations "turn the other cheek"
and "go the second mile" are no evidence that black
people should let white people beat the hell out of
them. We cannot use Jesus' behavior in the first century as a literal guide for our actions in the twentieth
century. To do so is to fall in the same trap that the
fundamentalists are guilty of. It destroys the freedom
of the Christian man, the freedom to make decisions
without an ethical guide from Jesus.

Scripture then is not a guide which makes our decisions for us. On the contrary, it is a theological source
because of its power to "renew for us the disclosure of
the holy which was the content of the primordial

revelation." [9] The God who is present today in our midst is the same God who revealed himself in Jesus Christ as witnessed in the Scriptures. By reading an account of God's activity in the world as recorded in Scripture, it is possible for a community in the twentieth century to experience the contemporary work of God in the world. The meaning of Scripture is not to be found in the words of Scripture as such but only in its power to point beyond itself to the reality of God's revelation; and in America, that means black liberation. Herein lies the key to the meaning of biblical inspiration. The Bible is inspired because through reading it a community can encounter the resurrected Christ and thus be placed in a state of freedom whereby it will be willing to risk all for earthly freedom.

6. *Tradition.* Tradition refers to the theological reflection of the church upon the nature of Christianity from the time of the early church to the present day. It is impossible for any student of Christianity to ignore tradition because the New Testament itself is a result of it. The possibility of going back to the Bible without taking into account the tradition which gave rise to it and which defines our contemporary evaluation of it is unthinkable; for tradition controls (in part) both our negative and positive thinking about the nature of the Christian gospel.

Though tradition is essential for any theological

[9] *Ibid.*

evaluation of Christianity, Black Theology is not un-
critical of it, particularly the history of western Christianity since the fourth century. The "conversion" of
Constantine to Christianity and his subsequent enact-
ment of it as the official religion of the Roman Empire
(replacing the public state sacrifices) raises some serious questions about Christendom, especially the possibility of its remaining true to its origin and task. It
could be argued that this is the beginning of the de-
cline of Christianity so evident in contemporary American society. Is it possible for the church to be the
church (*i.e.*, a church committed unreservedly to the
oppressed in society) and at the same time an integral
part of the societal structure? I think not. If the gospel
of Christ is the gospel of and for the oppressed in the
society, the church of Christ cannot be the religion of
the society. But it seems that the official church which
has been most responsible for the transmission of the
gospel tradition has played also the role as the political
enforcer of "law and order" against the oppressed by
divinely sanctioning the laws of the state and thus serving as the "redemptive" center of an established order.
The long bloody history of Christian anti-Semitism is a
prominent case in point.

The Protestant Reformation in the sixteenth century
did little to change this emphasis. Luther's identification with the oppressors in society enabled him to
speak of the state as a servant of God at the same time
the oppressed were being tortured by the state. It is

impossible for the oppressed who are seeking liberation to think of the state as God's servant. In most cases, the state is responsible for the condition of human enslavement and is thus the enemy of all who are interested in human freedom.

Luther's concern for "law and order" in the midst of human oppression is seriously questioned by Black Theology. While it may be doubtful whether his doctrine of the relation between church and state prepared the way for Hitler's genocide of the Jews in Europe, it did little to prevent it. In fact, his condemnation of the Peasant Revolt sounds very much like white churchmen's condemnation of ghetto rebellions.[10]

[10] I am not suggesting that Luther had no place in his theology for resisting the state. As P. S. Watson pointed out, Luther believed that it was the job of the preachers of the Word to rebuke rulers publicly when they failed in their duty. "Such rebuking Luther himself knew well how to undertake. Even in the case of the Peasants' Revolt, he laid the entire blame for the rising at the door of the Princes—W.M.L., IV, 220 ff.—whose sins he also frequently denounces elsewhere, and in no measured terms" (Watson, *The State as a Servant of God* [London: Society for Promoting Christian Knowledge, 1946], p. 65n.).

Black Theology can appreciate Luther's speaking out against the evils of the Princes (a trait that is typical of many theologians), but, and this is the problem with Luther, he was a "law and order" man even at the expense of the oppression of the poor. Watson reminds us of his unqualified insistence that "one must not resist the government with force, but only with knowledge of the truth; if it is influenced by it, well; if not, you are innocent and suffer wrong for God's sake." (Cited by Watson, *op. cit.*, p. 71n.). Now such advice will not go over well in the black community. Indeed it sounds too much like white ministers telling black people to be nonviolent while they enslave them. It could be that we can excuse Luther (after all, he lived in the sixteenth century!), but certainly not white religionists

The other Protestant reformers, especially Calvin and Wesley, did little to make Christianity a religion for the politically oppressed in the society. Though no man is responsible for everything that is done in his name, one may be suspicious of the easy affinity of Calvinism, capitalism, and slave trading.[11] John Wesley also said little about slaveholding and did even less.[12] We are told that Wesley's Methodism prevented a revolution in England, but I am not sure whether we should praise or condemn him on that account. The behavior of the white Methodist Church in America,

who use him as the guide for their thinking on the black revolution in America.

[11] See Max Weber, *The Protestant Ethic and the Spirit of Capitalism*, trans. by Talcott Parsons (New York: Charles Scribner's Sons, 1958), and J. R. Washington, *The Politics of God* (Boston: Beacon Press, 1967), Chapter IV.

[12] Of course, this is not to say that Wesley was completely silent on this issue. It was hard for any sensitive man during his time to ignore the question of slavery altogether. My point is simply this: in reading his sermons and other writings, one does not get the impression that slavery was one of the burning issues on Wesley's mind. Indeed, for Wesley Christianity seems to be primarily "personal" (a deliverance from sin and death) and not too political. His preoccupation with sanctification and what that entails seems to have distorted his picture of the world at large. Perhaps the later followers distorted the real Wesley by placing an undue emphasis on the "warm heart." But at least the Wesley that has come to us seems very white and quite British, and that ain't no good for black people who know that the Englishmen are the scoundrels who perfected the slave trade.

Black Theology must counsel black people to beware of the Wesley brothers and their concern for personal salvation, the "warm heart" and all that stuff. What black people do not need are warm hearts. Our attention must be elsewhere—say, the political, social and economic freedom of black people!

with its vacillation on slavery and colonization, is consistent with Wesley's less than passionate approach to the issues.

Black Theology believes that the spirit of the authentic gospel is often expressed by the "heretics" rather than the "orthodox" tradition. Certainly the so-called Radical Reformers were closer to the truth of Christianity in their emphasis on Christian discipleship through an identification with the oppressed of the land than was Luther, who called on the state to put down peasants.

Regarding what is often called tradition, Black Theology perceives *moments* of authentic identification with the ethical implications of the gospel of Christ, but they are rare. When Black Theology speaks of the importance of tradition, it focuses primarily on the history of the black church in America and secondarily on white western Christianity. It believes that the authentic Christian gospel as expressed in the New Testament is found more in the pre-Civil War black church than in its white counterpart. The names of Richard Allen, Daniel Payne, and Highland Garnet are more important in analyzing the theological implications of black liberation than Luther, Calvin, and Wesley. This is partially true because they are black but more importantly because inherent in their interpretation of the gospel is political, economic and social liberation. These men recognized the incompatibility between Christianity and slavery. While the white church in America was rationalizing slavery through clever exegesis, the black ministers were preaching freedom and equality.

The black church in America was founded on the belief that God condemned slavery and that Christian freedom meant political emancipation. Highland Garnet even argued that it was both a political and Christian right that slaves should rise in revolt against their white masters by taking up arms against them.

> Brethren, it is as wrong for your lordly oppressors to keep you in slavery as it was for the man-thief to steal our ancestors from the coast of Africa. You should therefore now use the same manner of resistance as would have been just in our ancestors when the bloody footprints of the first remorseless soul-thief was placed upon the shores of our fatherland.[13]

Black Theology is only concerned with that tradition of Christianity which is usable in the black liberation struggle. As it looks over the past, it asks: "How is the Christian tradition related to the oppression of black people in America?"

The Norm of Black Theology

In the previous section, we attempted to set forth the basic sources of Black Theology. It is appropriate

[13] Quoted in B. E. Mays, *The Negro's God* (New York: Atheneum, 1968), p. 46.

now to analyze the hermeneutical principle or norm which is operative in Black Theology as it makes a theological determination regarding the sources. Sometimes it is possible to perceive the norm of a particular theology through an evaluation of the selection and analysis of the sources; but this is not always true, since most theologies share common sources. As we have pointed out, the difference between Barth and Tillich does not lie in their choice of sources. The crucial difference is in their use of the sources, which is traceable back to their definition of the theological norm.

The theological norm is the hermeneutical principle which is decisive in specifying how sources are to be used by rating their importance and by distinguishing the relevant data from the irrelevant. For example, most theologians would agree that the Bible is important for the theological task. But there are sixty-six books in the Bible, and how are we going to decide which books are more important than others? The answers to this question range from the fundamentalist's verbal-inspiration view to the archliberal view that the Bible is merely one of many records of man's religious experiences. In all cases, the importance and use of the Bible are determined by the theological norm which is brought to the Scripture. Theologies with a kerygmatic consciousness would like to think that the norm arises from Scripture itself, but this is not always easy to determine. What is certain is that the theologian brings to the Scripture the perspective of a community, and what is to be hoped is that that community's concern is consistent with the concern of the community that gave us the Scriptures. It is the task of theology to keep these two communities (biblical and contemporary) in constant tension in order that we may be able to speak meaningfully about God in the contemporary situation.

Black Theology seeks to create a theological norm which is in harmony with the black condition and the biblical revelation. On the one hand, the norm must not be a private norm of a particular theologian but must arise from the black community itself. This means that there can be no norm for the black community which does not take seriously its reality in the world and what that means in a white racist society. Theology cannot be indifferent to the importance of blackness by making some kind of existential leap beyond blackness to an undefined universalism. It must take seriously the questions which arise from black-existence and not even try to answer white questions, questions coming from the lips of those who know oppressed existence only through abstract reflections.

If theology is to be relevant to the human condition which created it, it must relate itself to the questions which arise out of the community responsible for its reason for being. The very existence of Black Theology is dependent on its ability to relate itself to the human situation unique to oppressed men generally and black people particularly. If Black Theology fails to do this adequately, then the black community will and should destroy it. Black people have heard enough about God. What they want to know is what God has to say about the black condition. Or, more importantly, what is he doing about it? What is his relevance in the struggle against the forces of evil which seek to destroy black being? These are the questions which must shape the character of the norm of Black Theology.

On the other hand, Black Theology must not overlook the biblical revelation. This means that Black Theology should not devise a norm which ignores the encounter of the black community with the revelation of God. Whatever it says about liberation must be said in the light of the black community's experience of Jesus Christ. The failure of many black radicals to win the enthusiasm of the black community may be due to their inability to take seriously the religious character inherent in that community. It is not possible to speak meaningfully to the black community about liberation unless it is analyzed from a Christian perspective which centers on Jesus Christ. This accounts for the influence of Martin Luther King, Jr. As a prophet, with a charisma never before witnessed in this century, King preached black liberation in the light of Jesus Christ and thus aroused the spirit of freedom among black people. To be sure, one may argue that his method of nonviolence did not meet the needs of the black community in an age of Black Power; but it is beyond question that it was King's influence and leadership in the black community which brought us to the period in which we now live, and for that we are in his debt. His life and message demonstrate that the "soul" of the black community is inseparable from liberation but always liberation grounded in Jesus Christ. The task of Black Theology is to build on the foundation laid by King by recognizing the theological character of the black community, a community whose being is inseparable from liberation through Jesus Christ.

This is an awesome task for Black Theology. It is so easy to sacrifice one for the other. There is a tendency, on the one hand, to deny the relevance of Jesus Christ for black liberation especially in view of white prostitution of the gospel in the interest of slavery and white supremacy. One can be convinced that Jesus Christ is the white man's savior and god and thus can have nothing to do with black self-determination. And yet, what other name is there? It is the name of Jesus which has a long history in the black community. Black people know the source from which the name comes, but they also know the reality to which that name refers. Despite its misuse in the white community (even the devil is not prohibited from adopting God's name), the black community is convinced of the reality of Christ's presence and his total identification with the suffering of black people. They never believed that slavery was his will; and therefore every time a white master came to his death, black people believed

need to speak of both black liberation and JC

that it was the work of God inflicting his judgment in recompense for the sufferings of his people. Black Theology cannot ignore this spirit in the black community if it is going to win the enthusiasm of the community it serves.

Black Theology must also avoid the opposite error of speaking of Christ without reference to black liberation. The post-Civil War black church committed this error. It is so tempting to take the white Jesus who always speaks to black people in terms of white interest and power. He tells black people that love means turning the other cheek; that the only way to win your political freedom is through nonviolence; he even praises Martin Luther King, Jr., for his devotion to him, though he knows that King was always his enemy in spirit and that he chose King because he thought King was the least of the evils available. He tries to convince us that there is no difference between American democracy and Christian freedom, that violence is no way to respond to inhumanity. Black Theology must realize that the white Jesus has no place in the black community, and it is our task to destroy him. We must replace him with the Black Messiah, as Albert Cleage would say, a messiah who sees his existence as inseparable from black liberation and the destruction of white racism.

The norm of Black Theology must take seriously two realities, actually two aspects of a single reality: the liberation of black people and the revelation of Jesus Christ. With these two realities before us, what then is the norm of Black Theology? *The norm of all God-talk which seeks to be black-talk is the manifestation of Jesus as the Black Christ who provides the necessary soul for black liberation.* This is the hermeneutical principle for Black Theology which guides its interpretation of the meaning of contemporary Christianity. Black Theology refuses to accept any norm which does not focus on Jesus Christ, because he is the essence of the Christian gospel. But when we speak of the Christian gospel, we have merely scratched the surface by saying Jesus is at the center. It is so easy to make his name mean intellectual analysis, and we already have too much of that garbage in seminary libraries. What is needed is an application of the name to the concrete affairs of men. What does the name mean when black people are burning buildings and white people are responding with riot-police control? Whose side is Jesus on? The norm of Black Theology, which identifies revelation as a manifestation of the Black Christ, says that he is those very black men whom white society shoots and kills. The contemporary Christ is in the black ghetto, making decisions about white existence and black liberation.

Of course, this interpretation of theology will be strange to most white people and even some blacks will be made to wonder whether it is really true that

Christ is black. But the truth of the statement is not dependent on white or black affirmation, but on reality of Christ himself who is presently breaking the power of white racism. This and this alone is the norm for black-talk about God.

III

The Meaning
of Revelation

If we are going to speak about God and his movement in the world, it will be necessary to analyze the
methodological procedure which enables us to recognize his divine activity. This raises the question concerning the epistemological justification of the Christian faith. How do we know who God is or that he is
involved in our history? The rise of analytical philosophy, with its investigation of the relationship between
language and truth, has caused many theological
nightmares as religionists have sought to defend the
validity of theological speech. Religionists can be
thankful to the philosophy of language for subjecting
theological speech to the analytical test. Even though
we insist that truth is determined only by an oppressed
community asserting its existence in an oppressive

world, and not by an "uncommitted" philosopher of language applying an "objective" test, the logic of analytical philosophy does make us more sensitive in our use of language and forces us to subject our own language to tests devised by the community itself. Every community must ask, How do we know that our claims about God are valid? Every community which speaks about God must analyze the meaning of that speech by subjecting it to analytical tests which are in harmony with the perspective of the community. It is the task of theology to explicate coherently the validity of the community's claimed knowledge of God.

Of course, this does not mean that theology should be able to prove that Christianity is superior to other world views. In a world like ours with so many sharply divergent perspectives, it is not possible to know what constitutes proof or superiority. We are living in an immensely complex world, and our finite existence cannot qualify us to postulate absolute value judgments about concrete possibilities of operating in the world. We should be especially suspicious of the religious man who claims that his view of things is more just than others. In the words of Pascal, "Men never do evil so fully and so happily as when they do it for conscience's sake." [1] What authentic Christians know (and do not know—an element which enables them to act with *conviction* but never dogmatism) is their unwillingness to

[1] Quoted in Paul Oestreicher, ed., *The Christian Marxist Dialogue* (New York: The Macmillan Co., 1969), p. ix.

accept the world as it is. Children were not created for torture, and men and women were not created to have their dignity crushed. We believe that the Christian gospel offers men an authentic response to inhumanity by assuring them of God's participation against human suffering. The knowledge of God frees men to be all for the neighbor without having to worry about storing treasures on earth or living in such a way as to guarantee a heavenly treasure in the next life.

As we pointed out in an earlier chapter, the gospel offers no assurance of winning. Again, what could "winning" possibly mean? If it means what white people mean by it—an enslavement of human beings on the basis of white supremacy—then, "God deliver us!" The idea of winning is a hang-up of liberal whites who want to be white and Christian at the same time; but they fail to realize that this approach is a contradiction in terms—Christianity and whiteness are opposites. Therefore, when whites say, "That approach will not win out," our reply must be: "What the hell do you mean? Who's trying to win?" The only real question for Christians is whether their actions are in harmony with their knowledge of God. And the only people who are in a position to answer the question concerning the epistemological justification of the knowledge of God are the members of the community itself. Others, with some empathy, may evaluate the community's perspective intellectually, but they cannot tell the community what is or is not true and expect the community to take it seriously. This is especially true for white people who are in the habit of telling black people what is and is not the appropriate response to white racism, white religionists not excluded. The latter, intrigued by their own expertise in Christian theology, think they have the moral and intellectual right to determine whether black churches are Christian. They fail to realize that their analysis of Christianity is inseparable from their oppressor-mentality which shapes everything they say about God.

The development of the idea of Black Theology is an attempt of the black community itself to define what the knowledge of God means for its existence in a white racist society. To ask about the epistemological justification of our claim to the knowledge of God is to ask about the concept of revelation. When a religious community is asked, "How do you know that your assertions about God are valid?" the only reply is "We know because of revelation." Revelation then is the epistemological justification of a community's claims about ontological reality. Tillich, of course, is correct when he reminds us that "every epistemological assertion is implicitly ontological." [2] Nevertheless, it is necessary to make rational sense out of the community's ontological assertions, so that they themselves will understand more clearly the meaning of their commitment to the ultimate. Therefore, if the theologian is

[2] Tillich, *Systematic Theology*, Vol. I, p. 71.

going to make intelligible the community's view of God and man, it is necessary to begin with a rational analysis of revelation so that the presuppositional character of Christian theology will be clear from the outset.

American Theology and Revelation

In Protestant Christianity, because of the influence of the so-called Barthian school,[3] the first half of this century will be remembered for the radical reinterpretation of the idea of revelation. Before this period, revelation was largely understood as divine information *about* God communicated to man either through reason (natural theology) or through faith (assent to biblical truths). The major exception to this interpretation was Friedrich Schleiermacher's interpretation of religion as a "feeling of absolute dependence." Theology, according to him, rests neither on truths found by reason nor on authoritatively communicated truths of the Scripture but on the religious self-consciousness of the Christian community. For Schleiermacher, theology

[3] I realize that theological labels are grossly misleading, and this is especially true of the so-called Barthian camp. They have been called everything from "neo-fundamentalists" to "new reformation theologians." But theological labels fail to consider the radically different theological perspectives of such men as Barth, Tillich, Bultmann, Niebuhr and others. We only use the term "Barthian" as an easy method for describing the *new* emphasis on revelation which is common to them all, and not as a description of their world-views.

was an explication of the meaning of this communal self-consciousness.

This approach earned Schleiermacher the title "the father of modern Protestant theology," because his view transcended the old dichotomy between Protestant dogmatism and philosophic rationalism. But there were other problems with this view of the knowledge of God. Ludwig Feuerbach pointed out the dangers of this approach.[4] By using human self-consciousness as a point of departure for God-talk, theology gave credence to the Feuerbachian claim that theology is nothing but anthropology, the idea of God being a projection of man's view of his own greatness. Recent studies in Schleiermacher have challenged this view of him; but it is beyond question that he was the most influential religious thinker in the nineteenth century, and that was the century that put its confidence in man and human progress. We cannot help but think that Schleiermacher's anthropological point of departure was partly responsible for this. It certainly did not challenge it.

Through the rediscovery of Kierkegaard, the impact of World War I, the failure of the Social Gospel, and the irrelevancy of orthodox views of verbal infallibility of Scripture, the Barthians were led to a new understanding of God's revelation to man. All agreed that revelation had nothing to do with truths about God

[4] See *The Essence of Christianity*, trans. by George Eliot (New York: Harper and Brothers, 1957).

communicated through the church, Scripture, or reason. Revelation is rather the disclosure of God himself
in the person of Jesus Christ. Revelation is not a rational articulation of human self-consciousness, but an
existential encounter in a situation of concern, as Tillich would say. Of course, there were differences
among them in their views of revelation. Emil Brunner
preferred to speak of the divine-human encounter
which does not deny the reality of general revelation.
For Barth, revelation was the Wholly Other God de-
scending to man like a bolt from the blue, transforming
radically his human situation. Tillich wanted to preserve the cultural relevancy of revelation by emphasizing the "concrete situation of concern." For Bultmann,
with his existential orientation, revelation was the
means by which man attains his own authenticity. But
for all of these men revelation meant a manifestation of
God himself in human history.

Unfortunately the European analysis has done little
in helping American theology to focus on the central
meaning of God's revelation in this country. Barth,
Bonhoeffer and other members of the Confessing
Church of Germany were able to relate God's self-disclosure to the existing situation of oppression during
the reign of Hitler. Revelation meant that no human
order is synonymous with God's order, and that it is
better to choose death than obey the evils of the state.
Even Bultmann, with his view of revelation as essentially a spiritual self-understanding and not political

talk, spoke out against the dangers implied in Nazism. In a public lecture, May 2, 1933, he said:

> Ladies and gentlemen! I have made a point never to speak about current politics in my lectures, and I think I also shall not do so in the future. However, it would seem to me unnatural were I to ignore today the political situation in which we begin this new semester. The significance of the political happenings for our entire existence has been brought home to us in such a way that we cannot evade the duty of reflecting on the meaning of our theological work in this situation.[5]

He went on to emphasize the dangers in referring to the state as an ordinance of God. To know God as creator is to know the inherent potentiality and actuality of sin which characterizes every human act. Complete obedience belongs only to God and not the state.

What is strange, though perhaps understandable, is the silence of American theology regarding God's revelation and the oppressed of the land. Why is it that the idea of *liberation* (inseparable from the biblical view of revelation) is conspicuously absent among theological discussions about the knowledge of God? No sensitive religionist has endeavored to apply the contemporary manifestation of God's revelation to the situation of black people. To be sure, American religionists have

[5] *Existence and Faith, shorter writings of Rudolf Bultmann*, trans. by S. M. Ogden (New York: The World Publishing Co., 1960), p. 158.

informed us that God's revelation is a disclosure of himself to man in man's time, effecting man's salvation. But for some reason the contemporary significance of the biblical meaning has been sidestepped. It seems that white theology has made revelation and redemption into an esoteric word game without much meaning for the world at large. Some of Reinhold Niebuhr's early writings may be an exception, especially his *Moral Man and Immoral Society*.[6] But for the most part, theological talk in this country has been nothing but a participation in the structures of political oppression under the disguise of freedom and democracy. It is a sad fact that the most blatant expressions of human oppression (the enslavement of black Americans) have been overlooked in American theology. And because of that gross sin, it cannot be forgiven.

Black Theology and Revelation

Black Theology agrees with contemporary theology that God's self-disclosure is the distinctive characteristic of divine revelation. Divine revelation is not the rational discovery of God's attributes or assent to infallible biblical propositions, nor yet an aspect of human self-consciousness. Rather, revelation has to do with God himself as he is in his personal relationship with man, effecting his divine will in our history.

But Black Theology cannot stop here. There is a

[6] New York: Charles Scribner's Sons, 1932.

need to define revelation in such a manner that the definition will, on the one hand, retain the essence of the biblical emphasis and, on the other, be relevant to the situation of oppressed black people. In the zeal to be biblical, we cannot lose sight of the contemporary situation and what this situation means to the oppressed of the land. If we fail by ignoring the poor and the unwanted we become antibiblical. The racist will accept the view of revelation which stresses the self-disclosure of God as long as the interpretation remains antibiblical and thus does not challenge his right to define the limits of black humanity. The fact that the racist can also agree on this view of revelation means that there is something lacking in the contemporary interpretation of it.

According to Black Theology, revelation must mean more than just divine self-disclosure. Revelation is God's self-disclosure to man *in a situation of liberation*. To know God is to know of his activity of liberation on behalf of the oppressed. God's revelation means liberation, an emancipation from the political, economic and social structures of the society. This is the essence of the biblical revelation.

There is no revelation of God without a condition of oppression which develops into a situation of liberation. His revelation is only for the oppressed of the land. He comes to those who have been enslaved and abused and declares his complete identification with their situation, disclosing to them the rightness of their emancipation on their own terms. God not only reveals to the oppressed the divine right to break the chains by any means necessary, but also assures them that their work in their own liberation is God's own work.

When we apply this view of God's revelation to the existing situation of black people in America, we immediately realize that the black revolution in America is the revelation of God. Revelation means Black Power, *i.e.* the "complete emancipation of black people from white oppression by whatever means black people deem necessary." [7] It is black people telling white people where to get off, and a willingness to accept the consequences.

God's revelation has nothing to do with white suburban ministers admonishing their people to be nice to black people. It has nothing to do with voting for open occupancy or having a memorial service for Martin Luther King, Jr. God's revelation means a radical encounter with the structures of power which Martin King fought against to his death. It is what happens in a black ghetto when black people decide to strike against their enemies. In a word, God's revelation means *liberation*, nothing more and nothing less.

The Biblical View of Revelation

Black Theology's emphasis on liberation as an indispensable ingredient of revelation is inherently biblical.

[7] Cone, *Black Theology and Black Power*, p. 6.

The biblical emphasis on liberation may be approached through an analysis of the relationship of revelation, faith and history.

In the Bible revelation is inseparable from history and faith. History is the arena in which God's revelation takes place. Unlike many non-Christian religions, the God of the Bible is a God who makes his will and purpose known through his participation in human history. That is why Christianity has been described as a historical religion. It is a religion which affirms that we know who God is by what he does in the historical events of man. In fact, there is no revelation of God without history. The two are inseparable.

It is this realization that made Wright and Fuller entitle their book *The Book of the Acts of God* [8] and encouraged other biblical scholars to speak of Israelite history as "the history of Salvation." In the same vein Rudolf Bultmann's hermeneutical method of demythologizing [9] received some sharp criticism because it seemed to challenge the place of history in Christianity. Most scholars believe that it is not possible to retain the essence of biblical religion without seeing God as a God who is involved in the affairs of men.

It is important to note the history which God chose to disclose his will. God chose to make himself known

[8] New York: Doubleday and Co., 1957.
[9] See Rudolf Bultmann, "New Testament and Mythology," in H. W. Bartsch, ed., *Kerygma and Myth* (New York: Harper and Row, Publishers, 1961).

to an oppressed people, and the nature of his revelatory activity was synonymous with their emancipation. The Exodus of Israel from Egypt meant that God's revelation was an act of liberation. In this revelatory event, Israel not only came to know God as the liberator of the oppressed, but she also realized that her being as a people was inseparable from divine activity. Thus Yahweh was known primarily for what he did for Israel when other political powers threatened her existence as a community. The biblical writers expressed Israel's view of God's revelation by describing Yahweh as a war God.

> I will sing to the Lord, for he has triumphed gloriously;
> the horse and his rider he has thrown into the sea.
> The Lord is my strength and my song,
> and he has become my salvation;
> this is my God, and I will praise him,
> my father's God, and I will exalt him.
> The Lord is a man of war;
> the Lord is his name. (Exodus 15:1b–3)

In this passage God's revelation means political emancipation, which involves his destruction of the enemy. In view of God's overwhelming defeat of the Egyptians, a covenant is made with Israel. The covenant is an expression of God's identification with Israel and his will to be her God and she his people. The entire history of Israel is a history of what God has done, is doing, and will do in moments of oppression.

Though God acts in history, only the community of *faith* is able to perceive God's revelation. Revelation, in the biblical perspective, is inseparable from those with faith to perceive it. Faith then is the perspective which enables man to recognize God's actions in human history. All men could have seen the exodus of a small band of people from Egypt and their subsequent entering into the land of Canaan, thereby establishing themselves as a recognizable community from about the twelfth century B.C.; but only those with the faith of Israel would know that these events of liberation are the revelation of God himself. They did not happen by chance, and neither can they be explained in terms of man's capabilities. The only explanation in the eyes of Israel is Yahweh himself, who saw their affliction in Egypt, took pity on them, and set them free. This is Israel's faith, her way of interpreting her existence as a people. Faith then is the existential recognition of a situation of oppression and a participation in God's liberation.

By making revelation a historical happening, the Bible makes faith something other than an ecstatic feeling in moments of silent prayer, or an acceptance of inerrant propositions. Faith is the community's response to God's act of liberation. It is saying Yes to God and No to oppressors. Faith is the existential element in revelation, *i.e.*, the community's perception of their being and the willingness to fight against nonbeing.

It is not difficult to make a contemporary application of this view to the plight of black people today. Indeed it is difficult to ignore. How could we speak about God's revelation in the Exodus, the conquest of Palestine, the role of the Judges of Israel without seeing parallels in black history? In Israel the Judge was a charismatic leader, endowed with the spirit of Yahweh; he led his people in battle against the enemy. Is it really hard for us to believe that black examples of this would be Nat Turner, Denmark Vesey, and Malcolm X? These men represent the "soul" of blackness, and what black people mean by black liberation. They are the black judges endowed with the spirit of Yahweh for the sole purpose of creating the spirit of freedom among their people.

General and Special Revelation

In the history of theology, it is not uncommon to make a distinction between general revelation and special revelation. General revelation refers to the knowledge of God independent of the biblical revelation. Special revelation refers to the knowledge of God through biblical revelation, focusing primarily on Jesus Christ as the sole criterion for knowledge of God.

1. General Revelation. Every student of theology knows of Karl Barth's merciless attack on natural theology, which he believed failed to take due notice of the infinite qualitative distinction between God and man.

God is God and man is man, and there is a difference, according to Barth. Any form of natural theology which attempts to decide *a priori* what God ought to do is presumption, that is, sin. A passage from Barth's *Epistle to the Romans* reveals the vehemence of his rejection of natural theology.

> God, the pure and absolute boundary and beginning of all that we are and have and do; God, who is distinguished qualitatively from men and from everything human, and must never be identified with anything which we name, or experience, or conceive, or worship, as God; God, who confronts all human disturbance with an unconditional command "Halt," and all human rest with an equally unconditional command "Advance"; God the "Yes" in our "No" and the "No" in our "Yes"; the First and the Last, and, consequently, the Unknown, who is never a known thing in the midst of other known things; God, the Lord, the Creator, the Redeemer:—this is the living God.[10]

Barth is attacking any form of natural theology expounded by liberal theology, as well as all forms of mysticism, especially that form in which man sinks within himself to find God. In opposition to these views, he affirms that God and man are on different levels; they do not move in the same dimensions. If there is to be any relationship between the two, the initiative cannot come from man's side, as the exponents of natural theol-

[10] Barth, *Epistle to the Romans,* trans. by E. C. Hoskyns (London: Oxford University Press, 1933) pp. 330-331.

ogy assume, but it must be by God's coming down to man's level, since man cannot of himself ascend to God. "God must," writes Barth "strike down perpendicularly as the vertical line to the horizontal."

Some of Barth's colleagues thought the Swiss was going too far. Emil Brunner, once an avid follower, severed his ties with him on the issue of general revelation. If we are going to assess Barth's unequivocal stance on general revelation, it will be necessary to take into consideration the *times* in which he lived. His theological stand against general revelation took place during the 1920's and 1930's, the time of Hitler, Stalin and Roosevelt. It was a time when natural theology tended toward glorification of the state and the persecution of the Jews. It is noteworthy that when the world situation changed, Barth began to speak about the *Humanity of God*.[11] It was about the same time that black people in America and throughout the world began to affirm their being by striking against their oppressors.

The theoretical question "Is there knowledge of God independent of the Bible?" is irrelevant. It is not the theologian's task to settle logical problems unrelated to the affairs of men. It is his task to speak to his times, pointing to God's revelation in the events around him.

According to Black Theology, the idea of general revelation is primarily applicable to oppressed people. To the extent that we are creatures who rebel against un-

[11] Richmond: John Knox Press, 1960.

godly treatment, God has made himself known. All human acts against alien powers of enslavement are acts of God. We do not need to read the Bible to know that human enslavement is ungodly, and the slaves will do everything possible to break the chains. God has created all men in such a way that none will cooperate contentedly in their own oppression. We are not creatures who can be domesticated. In this sense, whether all men know what some Christians call special revelation, they nevertheless know God, *i.e.*, it is their identity with the divine that makes all slaves rebel against their masters.

Emil Brunner emphasized the idea of general revelation in order to make all men responsible for their sin.

We distinguish categorically: formally the *imago* is not in the least touched—whether sinful or not, man is a subject and is responsible. Materially the *imago* is completely lost, man is a sinner through and through and there is nothing in him which is not defiled by sin.[12]

For Black Theology this is especially applicable to oppressors. They are held accountable for their enslavement of the oppressed, and no amount of rational alibis can free them of this responsibility. But we have to be careful in trying to make this aspect of general revelation applicable to the oppressed. In what sense are the oppressed sinners?

[12] Emil Brunner, *Natural Theology*, trans. by Peter Frankel (London: The Centenary Press, 1946), p. 24.

In an attempt to speak to this question, we must point out quite clearly that the oppressors are in no position to speak about the sinfulness of the oppressed. Black Theology rejects categorically white comments about the sins of black people, suggesting that we are partly responsible for our plight. Not only does such talk provide an ungodly method for easing the guilt of white oppressors, but it also suggests that whites and blacks are one community. Sin is a concept which is only meaningful within the context of a Christian community. It is the community's recognition that they have lost their *identity* for being. Since whites and blacks do not share a common identity, white people cannot possibly know what sin is from a black perspective.

Black Theology does not deny that all men are sinners. What it denies is white reflections on the sin of black people. Only black people can speak about sin in a black perspective and apply it to black and white people. The latter's vision of reality is too distorted and renders them incapable of talking to the oppressed about their shortcomings.

According to Black Theology, the sin of the oppressed is not that they are responsible for their own enslavement—far from it. Their sin is that of trying to "understand" the enslaver, to "love" him on his own terms. As the oppressed community recognize their situation in the light of God's revelation, they know now that they should have killed him instead of "loving" him.

To summarize general revelation from the perspective of Black Theology, to say all men know God means that human oppression is contradictory to the idea of the holy, and every blow for liberation is the work of God. God has not left himself without a witness.

2. *Special Revelation.* Special revelation has always occupied the central role in Christian theology. It means that God has made himself known in the biblical history and decisively in Jesus Christ. It is this conviction that Karl Barth takes seriously by using Christology as the point of departure of his *Church Dogmatics.* God has revealed himself fully in the man Jesus so that the norm of all existence is determined exclusively by him. He is the revelation of God. For the oppressed this means that authentic movement in the world and one's rebellion against the enemy is found in Christ.

Gordon Kaufmann, who writes systematic theology with a historicist perspective, makes this comment: "To say God's act in Christ is revelatory . . . means that the event of Jesus Christ was an occurrence in and through which God spoke and man heard; that is, here God communicated himself with sufficient effectiveness that man was enabled to appropriate the meaning and respond to it, his existence thus being radically transformed." [13] When that existence is black existence, such an analysis has far-reaching implications. Through Christ black people are able to perceive the nature of black being and destroy the forces of nonbeing (white people). The transformed existence is the new sense of self-evaluation and a new determination to say No to oppressors, and mean it. This is the meaning of special revelation for Black Theology.

Bultmann's View of New Testament Revelation

Contemporary New Testament scholarship is indebted to Rudolf Bultmann and the form-critical school for seeking to make the New Testament Jesus relevant for today. Like Barth, Bultmann rejected the nineteenth-century liberal attempt to find the Jesus of history so that he (Jesus) could be our contemporary model for the "good" life. Using the hermeneutical method of demythologization, he destroyed all attempts to find the so-called historical Jesus. In his book entitled *Jesus and the Word,* he writes:

> I do indeed think that we can know almost nothing concerning the life and personality of Jesus, since the early Christian sources show no interest in either, are moreover

[13] Gordon Kaufmann, *Systematic Theology: A Historicist Perspective* (New York: Charles Scribner's Sons, 1968), p. 52.

fragmentary and often legendary; and other sources about Jesus do not exist.[14]

Destroying all attempts to locate the Jesus of history, Bultmann seeks to interpret the New Testament in such a way that we are forced to make the New Testament kerygma relevant to modern man's existential situation.

Thus, according to Bultmann, "Revelation is *an occurrence that puts me in a new situation as a self,* in which, to be sure, there is also given the possibility of knowledge (namely, about myself in my new situation). . . ." [15] There can be no revelation which does not provide man with an understanding of his own authenticity. He writes:

The meaning of revelation consists in its being the means whereby we achieve our authenticity, which we cannot achieve by our resources. Therefore, to know about revelation means to know about our own authenticity—and, at the same time, thereby to know our limitations.[16]

It is not hard to recognize the existentialist influences upon Bultmann's interpretation, especially that of Martin Heidegger. In his view, revelation is not an alien substance which descends on man's situation. It is

[14] New York: Charles Scribner's Sons, 1958, p. 8.

[15] Bultmann, *Existence and Faith,* trans. by Schubert Ogden (New York: The World Publishing Co., 1960), p. 59. Bultmann's italics.

[16] Bultmann, *op. cit.,* p. 92.

man coming to his own self-understanding whereby he sees both the freedom and the limits of his own existence. Revelation is self-knowledge, a knowledge in which man makes a decision about his own existence in the world. That is why Bultmann says revelation is a *"personal address."* There can be no revelation which does not involve an existential decision.

By interpreting revelation as a transformation of the self in an existential moment of decision, Bultmann is able to make it something other than a *past* event. "It is precisely an 'eschatological' fact, i.e., the kind of fact in which the world comes to an end." [17] This means that revelation "is understood in its true character only when it is understood as something that takes place in the present, in my particular present." [18] Bultmann believes that revelation becomes contemporary through the preaching of the Word in the form of an address. Here contemporary man has to make a decision: either live or die.

Black Theology can agree with some aspects of Bultmann's interpretation. The idea that revelation changes my own self-understanding is crucial for Black Theology and biblical revelation. It is impossible to view the Exodus as an act of God without at the same time seeing it as an act that changes Israel's view of herself as a people. The resurrection of Christ certainly

[17] *Ibid.*, p. 78.
[18] *Ibid.*, pp. 78-79.

changed the self-understanding of the disciples. When men encounter God's self-disclosure, they not only know who God is but also who they are. This is also what the Black Revolution in America is all about. It is not enough to say that God's revelation is a Christ-event; it is a *black-event,* *i.e.,* black people expressing their being in spite of 350 years of white oppression. This is the reality that shapes the black perspective. To know God is to know about ourselves, our beautiful black selves. This is what revelation means to black people. It is a contemporary decision about a contemporary event, the event of black and white beings.

Our major difficulty with Bultmann's view is that it does not take seriously the irreducibly historical character of revelation. If we do not keep revelation within the context of history, then we are free to make it whatever we please. History is inseparable from the biblical view of revelation. While history is not the "proof" of revelation, it is the context in which the man of faith perceives God's activity. Therefore, revelation is not only my own individualistic self-understanding; it is the self-understanding of a community which sees God at work in history.

Equally important, Bultmann's view fails to express the idea of *liberation.* Revelation is a historical liberation of an oppressed people from slavery. When oppressed people come to know who they are, they will not tolerate oppression. This is the key to self-understanding. This is what Paul Tillich calls the courage to be,[19] *i.e.*, the courage to affirm one's being in spite of those elements of existence which threaten being. It is the courage to be black in spite of white people. This is what revelation means in our times.

[19] See Tillich, *The Courage to Be* (New Haven: Yale University Press, 1952).

IV

God in Black Theology

The reality of God is presupposed in Black Theology. Black Theology is an attempt to analyze the nature of that reality, asking what we can say about the nature of God in view of his self-disclosure in biblical history and the oppressed condition of black people.

If we take the question seriously, it becomes evident that there is no simple answer to it. To speak of God and his participation in the liberation of the oppressed of the land is a risky venture in any society. But if the society is racist and also uses God-language as an instrument to further the cause of human humiliation, then the task of authentic theological speech is even more dangerous and difficult.

It is *dangerous* because the true prophet of the gospel of God must become both "anti-Christian" and "un-

107

patriotic." It is impossible to confront a racist society, with the meaning of human existence grounded in commitment to the divine, without at the same time challenging the very existence of the national structure and all of its institutions, especially the established church. All national institutions represent the interests of the society as a whole. We live in a nation which is committed to the perpetuation of white supremacy, and it will try to exterminate all who fail to assist it in this ideal. The genocide of the American Indian is evidence of that fact. Black Theology represents that community of black people who refuse to cooperate in the exaltation of whiteness and the degradation of blackness. It proclaims the reality of the biblical God who is actively destroying everything that is against the manifestation of human dignity among black people.

Because whiteness by its very nature is against blackness, the black prophet is a prophet of national doom. He proclaims the end of the "American Way," for God has stirred the soul of the black community, and now that community will stop at nothing to claim the freedom that is 350 years overdue. The black prophet is a rebel with a cause, the cause of over twenty-five million American blacks and all oppressed men everywhere. It is God's cause because he has chosen the blacks as his own. And he has chosen them not for redemptive suffering but for freedom. Black people are not elected to be Yahweh's suffering people. Rather we are elected because we are oppressed against our will and God's, and he has decided to make our liberation his own. We are elected to be free now to do the work of him who has called us into being, namely the breaking of the chains. The black theologian must assume the dangerous responsibility of articulating the revolutionary mood of the black community. This means that his speech about God, in the authentic prophetic tradition, will always move on the brink of treason and heresy in an oppressive society.

The task of authentic theological speech is *difficult* because all religionists in the society claim to be for God and thus for man. Even the executioners are for God. They carry out punitive acts against certain segments of society because "decent" people need protection against the undesirables. That is why blacks were enslaved and Indians exterminated—in the name of God and freedom. That is why today blacks are forced into ghettos and shot down like dogs if they raise a hand in protest. When George Washington, Thomas Jefferson, Lyndon Johnson, Richard Nixon and other "great" Americans can invoke the name of God at the same time they are defining the society for white people only, then Black Theology knows that it cannot approach the God-question too casually. It must ask, "How can we speak of God without being associated with the oppressors of the land?" Whiteness is so pervasive that the oppressors can destroy the revolutionary mood among the oppressed by introducing the complacent white God into the black community, thereby reducing the spirit of freedom.

Therefore if black people want to break the chains,

they must recognize the need for going all the way if liberation is to be a reality. The white God will point to a heavenly bliss as a means of directing black people away from earthly rage. Freedom comes when we realize that it is against our interests, as a self-determining black community, to point out the "good" elements in an oppressive structure. *There are no assets to slavery!* Every segment of the society participates in black oppression. To accept the white God, to see good in the evil, is to lose sight of the goal of the revolution—the destruction of everything "masterly" in the society. "All or nothing" is the only possible attitude for the black community.

Must We Drop God-language?

Realizing that it is very easy to be co-opted by the enemy and his God-language, it is tempting to discard all references to God and to seek to describe a way of living in the world that could not possibly be associated with "Christian" murderers. Some existentialist writers like Camus and Sartre have taken this course, and many black revolutionaries find this procedure appealing. Seeing the ungodly behavior of white churches and the timid, Uncle Tom approach of black churches, many black militants have no time for God and all that religious crap with its deadly prattle about loving your enemies and turning the other cheek.

Christianity, they argue, participates in the enslavement of black Americans. Therefore an emancipation from white oppression means also liberation from the ungodly influences of the white man's religion. This approach is certainly understandable, and the merits of the argument warrant a serious investigation of this claim. As black theologians seeking to analyze the meaning of black liberation, we cannot ignore this mood. Indeed, it is quite tempting intellectually to follow the procedure. Nevertheless two observations are in order at this juncture.

(1) Black Theology affirms that there is nothing special about the English word "God" in itself. What is important is the dimension of reality to which it points. The word "God" is a symbol that opens up depths of reality in the world. If the symbol loses its power to point to the meaning of black liberation, then we must destroy it. Black Theology asks whether the symbol God has lost its liberating power. Must we conclude that as a meaningful symbol the word "God" is hopelessly dead and thus cannot be resurrected? Certainly Black Theology realizes that, when a society performs all ungodly acts against the poor in the name of God, there may come a time when the oppressed might have to renounce all claims to "faith" in God in order to affirm authentic faith in him. Sometimes because of the very nature of oppressed-existence, the oppressed must define their being by negating everything the oppressors affirm, including belief in God. The oppressed

must demonstrate that all communications are cut off. In Camus's words: "There is, in fact, nothing in common between a master and a slave; it is impossible to speak and communicate with a person who has been reduced to servitude." [1] Therefore, the oppressed and the oppressors cannot possibly mean the same thing when they speak of God. The God of the oppressed is a God of revolution who breaks the chains of slavery. The oppressors' God is a God of slavery and must be destroyed along with the oppressors. The question then, as Black Theology sees it, is not whether black people believe in God, but whose God?

(2) In response to those inclined to drop God-language, Black Theology also believes that the destiny of black people is inseparable from the religious dimensions inherent in the black community. Theologically, one way of describing this reality is to call it general revelation. This means that all men have a sense of the presence of God, a feeling of awe, and it is precisely this experience that makes men creatures who always rebel against domestication. The black community is thus a religious community, a community that views its liberation as the work of the divine.

Here it is important to note that every significant black liberation movement has had its religious dimensions. Black liberation as a movement began with the pre-Civil War black churches who recognized that

[1] Albert Camus, *The Rebel*, trans. by Anthony Bower, Vintage Book V30 (New York: Random House, 1956), p. 283.

Christian freedom grounded in Jesus Christ was inseparable from civil freedom. That is why black preachers
were the leaders in the struggle for abolition of slavery,
and why southern slave owners refused to allow the es-
tablishment of the independent black churches in the
South. It is true, however, that the post-Civil War
black church lost its emphasis on civil freedom and
began to identify Christianity with moral purity. But
this does not mean that religion is irrelevant altogether; it only means that religion unrelated to black
liberation is irrelevant. To try to separate black liberation from black religion is a mistake, because black religion is authentic only when it is identified with the
struggle for black freedom. The influences of Marcus
Garvey, Elijah Muhammed, Malcolm X, and Martin
Luther King, Jr., demonstrate the role of religion in
the black community.

It is not the task of Black Theology to remove the influences of the divine in the black community. Its task
is to interpret the forces of black liberation as divine
activity. Black Theology must retain God-language despite its perils, because the black community perceives
its identity in terms of divine presence. Black Theology
cannot create new symbols independent of the black
community and expect black people to respond. It
must stay in the black community and get down to the
real issue at hand ("cutting throats" to use LeRoi Jones'
phrase) and not waste too much time discussing the legitimacy of religious language. The legitimacy of any

language, religious or otherwise, is determined by its usability in the struggle for liberation. That the God-language of white religion has been used to create a docile spirit among black people while whites aggressively attacked them is beyond question. But that does not mean that we cannot kill the white God, so that the God of black people can make his presence known in the black-white encounter. The white God is an idol, created by the racist bastards, and we black people must perform the iconoclastic task of smashing false images.

Hermeneutical Principle for the Doctrine of God

Every doctrine of God is based on a particular theological methodology. For instance, Karl Barth's theological point of departure is the Word of God as revealed in the man Jesus. We know who God is, according to Barth, because we know who Christ is. To look for the knowledge of God other than in Christ is to look in the wrong place, and thus end up constructing images which reflect human pride rather than divine revelation. "The knowledge of God occurs in the fulfillment of the revelation of His Word by the Holy Spirit. . . . ." [2]

Paul Tillich, on the other hand, does not share

---

[2] Barth, *Church Dogmatics*, Vol. II, Pt. 1, trans. by T. H. L. Parker, W. B. Johnston, Harold Knight, J. L. M. Haire (London: T. & T. Clarke, 1957), p. 3.

Barth's kerygmatic emphasis. His theological methodology is a "method of correlation," in which he seeks
to relate the changeless gospel to changing cultural situations. Culture, according to Tillich, is indispensable
for God-talk. Relying heavily on existential philosophy
and its analysis of the human condition (a condition
that is best explained in the word "estrangement"), Tillich describes God as being-itself, which provides the
only answer to man's estrangement from self and the
neighbor. Since being-itself is free from the threat of
nonbeing or nothingness, it is the source of man's courage, which is man's ability to affirm his being in spite
of the presence of nonbeing. Therefore God is a symbolic word pointing to the dimension of reality which
is the answer to the human condition.

Since the perspective of Black Theology differs from
both Barth and Tillich, there is also a difference in its
approach to the doctrine of God. The point of departure of Black Theology is the biblical God as he is related to the black liberation struggle. It asks, "How do
we *dare* speak of God in a suffering world, a world in
which blacks are humiliated because they are black?"
This question, which occupies the central place in our
theological perspective, forces us to say nothing about
God that does not participate in the emancipation of
black people. God-talk is not Christian-talk unless it is
directly related to the liberation of the oppressed. Any
other talk is at best an intellectual hobby, and at worst
blasphemy.

There are then two hermeneutical principles which

are operative in Black Theology's analysis of the doctrine of God. (1) The Christian understanding of God arises from the biblical view of revelation, a revelation of God that takes place in the liberation of oppressed Israel and is completed in his becoming man in Jesus Christ. This means that whatever is said about the nature of God and his being-in-the-world must be based on the biblical account of God's revelatory activity. We are not free to say anything we please about him. While Scripture is not the only source that helps us to recognize divine activity in the world, it cannot be ignored if we intend to speak of the Holy One of Israel.

(2) The doctrine of God in Black Theology must be the God who is participating in the liberation of the oppressed of the land. This hermeneutical principle arises out of the first. Because God has made himself known in the history of oppressed Israel and decisively in the Oppressed One, who is Jesus Christ, it is impossible to say anything about him without seeing him as being involved in the contemporary liberation of all oppressed people. The God in Black Theology is the God of and for the oppressed of the land who makes himself known through their liberation. Any other view is a denial of the biblical revelation.

New Wine in New Wineskins

Because Black Theology is the theology of black liberation, it must break with traditional theological speech when that speech softens the drive for black self-determination. It cannot run the risk of putting "new wine into old wineskins" (Mark 2:22). When Jesus used the phrase, he was referring to the Kingdom of God and its relationship to the conventional Judaism of his time.

When the black theologian analyzes the doctrine of God, seeking to relate it to the emerging black revolution in America, he must be especially careful not to put this new wine (the revelation of God as expressed in Black Power) into old wineskins (white folk-religion). Black Theology's view of God must be sharply distinguished from white distortions about God. This does not mean that Black Theology rejects white theology entirely. Unfortunately, this cannot be done, since oppression always means that the communication skills of an oppressed community are determined to a large degree by the oppressors. That is precisely the meaning of oppression! Since black theologians are trained in white seminaries and white thinkers make decisions about the structure and scope of theology, it is not possible for black religionists to separate themselves immediately from white thought.

When Jesus spoke of his message of the Kingdom as new wine, it did not mean a total rejection of Judaism in the first century. What he meant was that the revolutionary message cannot be determined by the possibilities available in the old structure.

Similarly since our knowledge about Christianity

came from white oppressors, Black Theology's view of God is in part dependent on white theologians, but this does not mean white theologians set the criteria for Black Theology. Liberation means that the oppressed must define the structure and scope of reality for themselves without taking their cues from the oppressors. If there is one brutal fact that the centuries of white oppression have taught black people, it is that white people are rendered incapable of making any valid judgment about human existence. The goal of Black Theology is the destruction of everything *white* so that black people can be liberated from alien gods. The God of black liberation will not be confused with the bloodthirsty white idol. Black Theology must show that the God of black people has nothing to do with the God worshipped in white churches whose primary purpose is to sanctify the racism of whites and to daub the wounds of blacks. Putting new wine in new wineskins means that Black Theology's view of God has nothing in common with those who pray for an American victory in Vietnam or a "cool" summer in the ghetto.

Black Theology's refusal to put new wine in old wineskins also means that it will show that the God of the black community cannot be confused with the God of white seminaries. With their intellectual expertise, it is inevitable that white scholars fall into the racist error of believing that they have the right to define what is and what is not proper religious talk. Since they have read so many of their own books and heard themselves talk so often, it is not surprising that they actually believe most of the garbage they spout out about God. They therefore think that all authentic God-talk must meet their approval before it can be called theology. But Black Theology rejects their standards, for we know they speak for the oppressors, and thus will inevitably analyze the nature of God in the interest of white society as a whole.

Black Theology must also be suspicious of so-called white revolutionary theologians. What is most disturbing about their self-proclaimed identification with Black Power is their inability to let *us* speak for ourselves. They still insist on defining what Black Power is, and not only in private conversations but also in print. And to make it worse, they invariably miss the whole point regarding Black Power. They should know by now that, in view of white brutality against blacks and the church's participation in it, no white man who is halfway sensitive to black self-determination should have the audacity to speak for black people. That is the problem! *Too many whites think they know how we feel about them.* If whites were really serious about their radicalism in regard to the black revolution and its theological implications in America, they would keep silent and take instructions from black people. Only black people can speak about God as he is related to their liberation. And those who wish to join us in this divine work must be willing to lose their white identity —indeed destroy it.

Black Theology's emphasis also rejects any identification with the recent "death of God" theology. The death-of-God question is a white issue which arises out of the white experience. Questions like "How do we find meaning and purpose in a world in which God is absent?" are questions of an affluent society. Whites may wonder how to find purpose in their lives, but our purpose is forced upon us. We do not want to know how we can get along without God, but how we can survive in a world permeated with white racism.

God Is Black

Because black people have come to know themselves as *black,* and because that blackness is the cause of their own love of themselves and hatred of whiteness, God himself must be known only as he reveals himself in his blackness. The blackness of God, and everything implied by it in a racist society, is the heart of Black Theology's doctrine of God. There is no place in Black Theology for a colorless God in a society when people suffer precisely because of their color. The black theologian must reject any conception of God which stifles black self-determination by picturing God as a God of all peoples. Either God is identified with the oppressed to the point that their experience becomes his or he is a God of racism. Authentic identification, as Camus pointed out, is not "a question of psychological identification—a mere subterfuge by which the individual imagines that it is he himself who is being offended." It is "identification of one's destiny with that of others and a choice of sides." [3] Because God has made the goal of black people his own goal, Black Theology believes that it is not only appropriate but necessary to begin the doctrine of God with an insistence on his blackness.

The blackness of God means that God has made the oppressed condition his own condition. This is the essence of the biblical revelation. By electing Israelite slaves as his people and by becoming the Oppressed One in Jesus Christ, God discloses to men that he is known where men experience humiliation and suffering. It is not that he feels sorry and takes pity on them (the condescending attitude of those racists who need their guilt assuaged for getting fat on the starvation of others); quite the contrary, his election of Israel and incarnation in Christ reveal that the *liberation* of the oppressed is a part of the innermost nature of God himself. This means that liberation is not an afterthought, but the essence of divine activity.

The blackness of God then means that the essence of the nature of God is to be found in the concept of liberation. Taking seriously the Trinitarian view of the

[3] Camus, *op. cit.*, pp. 16, 17.

122   A *Black Theology of Liberation*

Godhead, Black Theology says that as Father, God identified with oppressed Israel participating in the bringing into being of this people; as Son, he became the Oppressed One in order that all may be free from oppression; as Holy Spirit, he continues his work of liberation. The Holy Spirit is the Spirit of the Father and the Son at work in the forces of human liberation in our society today. In America, the Holy Spirit is black people making decisions about their togetherness, which means making preparation for an encounter with white people.

It is Black Theology's emphasis on the blackness of God that distinguishes it sharply from contemporary white views of God. White religionists are not capable of perceiving the blackness of God because their satanic *whiteness* is a denial of the very essence of divinity. That is why whites are finding and will continue to find the black experience a disturbing reality. White theologians would prefer to do theology without reference to color, but this only reveals how deeply racism is embedded in the thought forms of this culture. To be sure, they would *probably* concede that the concept of liberation is essential to the biblical view of God. But it is still impossible for them to translate the biblical emphasis on liberation to the black-white struggle today. Invariably they quibble on this issue, moving from side to side, always pointing out the dangers of extremism on both sides. (In the black community, we call this shuffling.) They really cannot make a decision, because it has been made already for them. The way in which scholars would analyze God and black people was decided when black slaves were brought to this land, while churchmen sang "Jesus, Lover of My Soul." Their attitude today is no different from that of the Bishop of London who assured the slaveholders that

> Christianity, and the embracing of the Gospel, does not make the least Alteration in Civil property, or in any Duties which belong to Civil Relations; but in all these Respects, it continues Persons just in the same State as it found them. The Freedom which Christianity gives, is a Freedom from the Bondage of Sin and Satan, and from the dominion of Man's Lust and Passions and inordinate Desires; but as to their outward Condition, whatever that was before, whether bond or free, their being baptized and becoming Christians, makes no matter of change in it.[4]

Of course white theologians today have a "better" way of putting it, but what difference does that make? It means the same thing to black people. "Sure," as the so-called radicals would say, "God is concerned about black people." And then they go on to talk about God and secularization or some other white problem unrelated to emancipation of black people. This style is a contemporary white way of saying that "Christianity . . . does not make the least alteration in civil property."

[4] Quoted in H. Richard Niebuhr, *The Social Sources of Denominationalism* (Cleveland: Meridian Books, 1929), p. 249.

In contrast to this racist view of God, Black Theology proclaims his blackness. People who want to know who God is and what he is doing must know who black people are and what they are doing. This does not mean lending a helping hand to the poor and unfortunate blacks of the society. It does not mean joining the war on poverty! Such acts are sin offerings that represent a white way of assuring themselves that they are basically a "good" people. Knowing God means being on the side of the oppressed, becoming *one* with them and participating in the goal of liberation. *We must become black with God!*

It is to be expected that white people will have some difficulty with the idea of "becoming *black* with God." The experience is not only alien to their existence as they know it to be, it appears to be an impossibility. "How can *white* people become black?" they ask. This question always amuses me because they do not really want to lose their precious white identity, as if it is worth saving. They know, as everyone in this country knows, a black man is anyone who says he is black, despite his skin color. In the literal sense a black man is anyone who has "even one drop of black blood in his veins."

But "becoming black with God" means more than just saying "I am black," if it involves that at all. The question "How can white people become black?" is analogous to the Philippian jailer's question to Paul and Silas, "What must I do to be saved?" The implica-

tion is that if we work hard enough at it, we can reach
the goal. But the misunderstanding here is the failure
to see that blackness or salvation (the two are synonymous) is the work of God and not man. It is not something we accomplish; it is a gift. That is why they said,
"Believe in the Lord Jesus and you will be saved." To
believe is to receive the gift and utterly to reorient
one's existence on the basis of the gift. The gift is so
unlike what humans expect that when it is offered and
accepted, we become completely new creatures. This is
what the Wholly Otherness of God means. God comes
to us in his blackness which is wholly unlike whiteness,
and to receive his revelation is to become black with
him by joining him in his work of liberation.

Even some black people will find this view of God
hard to handle. Having been enslaved by the God of
white racism so long, they will have difficulty believing
that God is identified with their struggle for freedom.
Becoming one of his disciples means rejecting whiteness and accepting themselves as they are in all their
physical blackness. This is what the Christian view of
God means for black people.

The Love and Righteousness of God

The theological statement "God is love" is the most
widely accepted assertion regarding the nature of God.
All theologians would agree that it is impossible to

speak of the Christian understanding of God without affirming the idea of love as essential to his nature. Anders Nygren's *Agape and Eros* [5] is the classical treatment of the subject, and he shows, perhaps conclusively, that agape is inseparable from the authentic Christian view of God. When religionists deviated from the agape-motif, the result was always a distortion of the authentic Christian conception of God.

Though religionists have agreed that love is indispensable to the Christian view of God's nature, there has been much disagreement on how the idea of the *wrath* of God is reconciled with his love. Marcion was one of the first to face this problem head-on. According to him, it is impossible to reconcile the Old Testament idea of the righteous God with the New Testament idea of the love of God.[6] The concept of law (nomos) is a complete denial of love (agape). Marcion's solution was to insist that the gospel of Christ is completely new and thus has nothing to do with the concept of righteousness (including wrath) as presented in the Old Testament. This led him to posit two Gods, the Creator God of the Old Testament who stressed obedience to the law of righteousness and the Redeemer God of the New Testament who is the "good" God, the God of love. Interpreting Marcion's view, Nygren writes:

[5] Trans. by P. S. Watson (Philadelphia: The Westminster Press, 1953).
[6] This follows Nygren's view of Marcion; *Agape and Eros*, pp. 316–34.

The message of Christ is marked by the spontaneous love and mercy of the Highest God, shown to strangers, unmotivated and uncalculated. In the Old Testament, on the other hand, man's relation to God is dominated by the idea of retribution, of reward and punishment.[7]

It is to be expected that the church would reject Marcion's view since the early Christian community did not understand its existence as being completely new in the sense of negating the God of the Old Testament. They believed that they were the authentic continuation of the Old Israel and not its denial. Christ, therefore, did not destroy the Old Testament; he fulfilled it.

While the church rejected Marcion's sharp dichotomy between the Old Testament view of God's righteousness and the New Testament view of God's love in Jesus Christ, there is still much confusion about the precise relationship between the two "symbols" [8] when applied to God's nature. The most common procedure is to emphasize God's love as the dominant motif of Christianity and then interpret God's righteousness in the light of it. But this approach fails to take seriously the concept of God's righteousness and tends to make

[7] *Ibid.*, p. 321.

[8] I use "symbols" instead of "attributes" because I agree with Tillich and others who suggest that the phrase "attributes of God" is misleading. It suggests the idea of substance or property which God has. God is not an object, and thus cannot be referred to as such. "Symbol," though it has its weakness, is a better word for expressing the Being of God in the world.

God's love mere sentimentality. By emphasizing the love of God to the exclusion of a meaningful encounter of God's righteousness, we could argue that the approach is basically Marcionite, except that Marcion was more honest. Marcion claimed that the idea of righteousness is *basic* to the Old Testament view of God, and he was right in this. He further suggested that the idea of love as revealed in Christ is a negation of the Old Testament view of righteousness, and he was wrong in this. But most religionists, while rejecting the Marcion dichotomy, proceed to analyze the concept of the love of God without relating it to his righteousness. Marcion's position presents us with two alternatives. Either we agree with him and his view of the two Gods, Righteousness and Love, or we affirm the basic oneness of his righteousness and love, and that means that God's love is inexplicable without equal emphasis on his righteousness and vice versa. Contemporary theology seems to want to have the cake and eat it too, that is, reject the Marcionite view and also accept a view of love that ignores righteousness, and that is not possible.

Gordon Kaufmann's recent work, *Systematic Theology: A Historicist Perspective*, seems to be open to this criticism. Particularly concerned about protecting the idea of love in God's nature, Kaufmann says that it is improper to speak of the "wrath" of God as an expression of the being of God. While love is essential, the idea of wrath is an expression of the disobedience of

man and can be understood only by looking at man's
nature and not God's.

> The wrath of God is a symbol more appropriate to dis-
> cussion of the nature (and plight) of *man* than God. . . .
> The man hanging on the cross . . . reveals God's nature
> as long-suffering love, not vengeance or wrath in any
> sense. . . . Hence, in our direct exposition of the doc-
> trine of God such symbols as "wrath" would only be mis-
> leading and should be avoided: God reveals himself as
> love and faithfulness, and this it is that we must seek to
> grasp here.[9]

Black Theology agrees that the idea of love is indispensable to the Christian view of God. The Exodus,
the call of Israel into being as the people of the covenant, the gift of the Promised Land, the rise of prophecy, the Second Exodus and above all the incarnation
reveal God's self-giving love to oppressed man. We do
not read far in the biblical tradition without recognizing that the God-man fellowship is to be understood
exclusively in terms of what God does for man and not
what man does for himself or for God. That is why
Nygren is correct in describing God's agape as the "ini-
tiation of the fellowship with God," [10] and why it is appropriate for Barth to emphasize the complete freedom
of God in the divine-human encounter. If the incarna-

---

[9] Kaufmann, *Systematic Theology: A Historicist Perspective* (New
York: Charles Scribner's Sons, 1968), p. 154.

[10] Nygren, *op. cit.*, p. 80.

tion means anything in Christian theology, it must mean that "God so loved the world that he gave his only Son, that whoever believes in him should not perish but have eternal life" (John 3:16).

The love of God is the heart of the Christian gospel. As the writer of I John puts it, "God is love" (4:8, 16). Commenting on the theological implications of this phrase, C. H. Dodd writes:

> To say "God is love" implies that *all* His activity is loving activity. If He creates, He creates in love; if He rules, He rules in love; if He judges, He judges in love. All that He does is the expression of His nature which is —to love.[11]

Black Theology then asks not whether love is an essential element of the Christian interpretation of God, but whether the love of God itself can be properly understood without focusing equally on the biblical view of God's righteousness. Is it possible to understand what God's love means for the oppressed without making *wrath* an essential ingredient of that love? What could love possibly mean in a racist society except the righteous condemnation of everything white? Most theological treatments of God's love fail to place the proper emphasis on God's wrath, suggesting that love is completely self-giving without any demand for obe-

[11] C. H. Dodd, *The Johannine Epistles* (New York: Harper and Brothers, 1946), p. 110.

dience. Bonhoeffer called this "cheap grace." He writes:
"Cheap grace means grace as a doctrine, a principle, a
system. It means forgiveness of sins proclaimed as a
general truth, the love of God taught as the Christian
'conception' of God." [12]

The difficulty with Kaufmann's view and others like
his is not so much his explicit statements but their false
implications. By removing wrath as a symbol of the nature of God, his interpretation weakens the central
biblical truth about God's liberation of the oppressed
from the oppressors. A God without wrath does not
plan to do too much liberating, for the two concepts
belong together. A God minus wrath seems to be a
God who is basically not against anybody. All we have
to do is to behave nicely, and everything will work out
all right. But such a view of God leaves us in doubt
about God's role in the black-white struggle. Black people want to know whose side God is on and what kind
of decision he is making about the Black Revolution. We
will not accept a God who is on everybody's side—
which means that he loves everybody in spite of who
they are, and is working (through the acceptable chan-
nels of the society, of course) to reconcile all people to
himself.

Black Theology cannot accept a view of God which
does not represent him as being for blacks and thus
against whites. Living in a world of white oppressors,

[12] Dietrich Bonhoeffer, *The Cost of Discipleship* (New York: The
Macmillan Co., 1961), p. 35.

black people have no time for a neutral God. The brutalities are too great and the pain too severe, and this means we must know where God is and what he is doing in the revolution. There is no use for a God who loves whites the *same* as blacks. We have had too much of white love, the love that tells blacks to turn the other cheek and go the second mile. What we need is the divine love as expressed in Black Power which is the power of black people to destroy their oppressors, here and now, by any means at their disposal. Unless God is participating in this holy activity, we must reject his love.

The interpretation of God's love without righteousness also suggests that white "success" is a sign of God's favor, of his love. Kaufmann's view is open to the ungodly assumption that all is well with the way whites live in the world, because God loves them, and their material success is the evidence. But according to Black Theology, it is blasphemy to say that God loves white people unless that love is interpreted as his wrathful activity against them and everything that whiteness stands for in this society. If the wrath of God is his almightly No against man's Yes, then black people want to know where the No of God is today in white America. We believe that the black community's No as expressed in the black revolution is God's No, showing his rejection of the oppressors and his acceptance of the oppressed.

Kaufmann's view also suggests that there is knowl-

edge of God as he is in himself. Theologically this
seems impossible. We can only know God in his relation to man, or more particularly in his liberating activity on behalf of oppressed man. The attempt to analyze God independently of his liberating work is
analogous to the theological attempt to know man *before* the fall. The fall itself renders such knowledge impossible, since there is no way to get behind the
human condition as we know it to be. The limitation of
man's knowledge is equally true in regard to God as he
is in himself. We are not permitted to transcend our finiteness and rise to a vision of God unrelated to the
human condition. If this is true, what merit is there in
saying that God's wrath is not a part of his nature? If
God is a God of the oppressed of the land as the revelation of Christ discloses, then wrath is an indispensable element for describing the scope and meaning of
his liberation of the oppressed. The wrath of God is the
love of God in regard to the forces against his liberation of the oppressed.

Love without righteousness is unacceptable to black
people because this view of God is a product of the
minds of enslavers. By emphasizing the complete self-
giving of God in Christ without seeing also the content
of righteousness, the oppressors can then request the
oppressed to do the same for the oppressors. If God
gives himself without obligation, then in order to be
Christian, men must give themselves to the neighbor in
like manner. Since God has loved us in spite of our re-

volt against him, to be like God we too must love those who revolt against or enslave us. For black people this means letting white people crowd us in ghettos where rats and filth eat away at our being and not raising a hand against them. But this view of love places no obligation on the white oppressors. The existing laws of the society protect them, and their white skins are badges of acceptance. In fact, they are permitted to do whatever they will against black people, assured that God loves them as well as the people they oppress. Love means that God will accept the whites, and blacks will not seek reprisal.

Black Theology rejects this view, saying that the man who oppresses is in no position to define what love is. How could white scholars know that love means turning the other cheek since they have never had to do so? Only the man who is in the oppressed condition can know what his love-response ought to be to his oppressors. The oppressors certainly cannot answer that question for him! It is this fact that renders all white intellectual disputation about black people and God a religious lie. If the oppressors themselves, who claim to be followers of the love-ethic, would actually adhere to their own analysis, then the oppressed-condition would no longer exist. There is something demonic about white people who have the protection of the state but advise blacks to go the second mile for them. Since they have not even moved an inch for black people, how can they claim to be speaking from a common perspective called Christianity?

It takes a special kind of reasoning to conclude that God's love means that he is no respecter of persons in a society filled with hate where some men think they have the right to define the course of human history. Ungodly in their very relationship to black people, they want to tell us what God's love means. There is only one explanation for this attitude. They are white and can think only like white people, even in reference to God. How else do we explain that the white theologian's view of God's love invariably coincides with or complements the structure by making blacks complacent and obedient to white enemies? Can they really expect blacks to take them seriously?

The black theologian rejects the oppressor's view of God's love, because he represents a people who share Fanon's feelings about the world.

All the native has seen in his country is that they can freely arrest him, beat him, starve him: and no professor of ethics, no priest has ever come to be beaten in his place, nor to share their bread with him. As far as the native is concerned, morality is very concrete; it is to silence the settler's defiance, to break his flaunting violence—in a word, to put him out of the picture.[13]

[13] Frantz Fanon, *The Wretched of the Earth*, trans. by Constance Farrington (New York: Grove Press, 1963), p. 36.

Black Theology will accept only a love of God which participates in the destruction of the white enemy. With Fanon, Black Theology takes literally Jesus' statement, "the last will be first, and the first last." Black Power "is the putting into practice of this sentence." [14]

Black people cannot adhere to a view of God that will weaken their drive for liberation. This means that in a racist society, we must insist that God's love and his righteousness are two ways of talking about the same reality. Righteousness means that he is doing his black thing and love means that he is doing it in the interests of both black and white people. The blackness of God points to the righteousness of God, as well as his love.

Paul Tillich, in another connection, has placed a similar emphasis. Though he refuses to say that wrath is a part of God's being, it is to his credit that he has insisted that divine love and justice should not be separated. "Justice," he writes, "is that side of love which affirms the independent right to object and subject within the love relation." Since love is the reunion of the estranged, it "does not destroy the freedom of the beloved and does not violate the structures of the beloved's individual and social existence." [15] This means that justice is the structure necessary for man's expression of his freedom. To be God, God must protect both

[14] *Ibid.*, p. 40. Of course, Fanon was speaking in the context of decolonization.

[15] Tillich, *Systematic Theology*, Vol. I, p. 282.

the freedom and the structure of human behavior. That is why Tillich rejects sentimental misinterpretations of love as emotion, which suggest that there is a conflict between divine love and its relationship to power and justice. The three are inseparable, according to Tillich. He writes:

It must be emphasized that it is not divine power as such which is thought to be in conflict with the divine love. The divine power is the power of being-itself, and being-itself is actual in the divine life whose nature is love. A conflict can be imagined only in relation to the creature who violates the structure of justice and so violates love itself. When this happens . . . judgment and condemnation follow. . . . Condemnation then is not the negation of love but the negation of the negation of love.[16]

What then can we conclude about the meaning of God's love in a racist society? Using blackness as the point of departure, Black Theology believes the love of God to man is revealed in his willingness to become black. His love is incomprehensible apart from blackness. This means that to love black people he takes on black oppressed existence, becoming one of us. He is black because he loves us; and he loves us because we are black.

Righteousness is that side of God's love which expresses itself through black liberation. He makes black

[16] *Ibid.*, p. 283.

what men have made white. Righteousness is that aspect of God's love which prevents his love from being equated with sentimentality. Love is not accepting whiteness or overlooking white racism. To love is to make a decision against white people. Since love means that God meets our needs, God's love for white people could only mean wrath, that is, a destruction of their whiteness and a creation of blackness.

For Black Theology love cannot be discussed in the abstract. It must be concrete because black suffering is utterly concrete. Black suffering is white people making decisions about our place in the world, telling us what we can or cannot do in the society. Love must be brought down to this level, the reality of white inhumanity against the black community. As Fanon says, "no phraseology can be a substitute for reality." [17] That is why Black Theology says that God's love is God's liberation of black people as expressed in Black Power.

Traditional Theological Language and the Black God

One of the major tasks of Black Theology is that of making sense out of the traditional theological talk about God. It asks, in regard to every theological assertion, "What are its implications for the oppressed?" Or, more specifically, "Does it have any meaning in the

[17] Fanon, *op. cit.*, p. 36.

struggle for black liberation in America?" Believing that the biblical God makes himself known through the liberation of the oppressed, Black Theology's analysis of God begins with an emphasis on his blackness.

But now we must ask, How is the concept of the blackness of God related to such traditional divine symbols as creator, transcendence, immanence and providence?

1. God as Creator. The biblical view of God as creator is expressed in the priestly assertion, "In the beginning God created the heavens and the earth" (Genesis 1:1). To speak of God as creator means that the world and everything that is *is* because of the creative will of God. In traditional theological language, God as creator expresses his aseity, that is, the total independence of God from his creation. God is self-existent, meaning that the source of his existence is found in himself.

In order to emphasize the absolute sovereignty of God over his creation, traditional theology introduced the idea of creation out of nothing (*ex nihilo*). The purpose is to deny that God used an eternal substance (as in Plato) in the creation of the universe. The existence of an eternal substance would compromise the complete Lordship of God over his creation. God is fully free, Being without limitations.

Black Theology is not interested in debating the philosophical and theological merits of God's aseity except as it can be related to the earthly emancipation of the oppressed. What has the idea of God's self-existence to

do with the existence of the oppressed? First it is necessary to point out that the biblical view of God as creator is not a paleontological statement about the nature
and origin of the universe, but a theological assertion
about God and his relationship to the oppressed of the
land. It is important to remember that the priestly narrative was put together during the Babylonian exile as
an attempt to make theological sense of Israel's history
as an oppressed people. Therefore, it is impossible to
remain faithful to the biblical viewpoint without seeing
the doctrine of creation as a statement about God and
the oppressed of the land. God as creator means that
man is a creature; man's source for meaning and purpose in the world is not found in his oppressors but in
God himself. This view of God undoubtedly accounts
for Israel's exclusivism in a situation of political oppression.

Though white theologians have emphasized that
God as creator is a statement about the God-man relationship, they have not pointed out the political implications of this theological truth for black people. God
as creator has not been related to the oppressed in the
society. If creation "involves a bringing into existence
of something that did not exist before," [18] then to say
God is creator means that *my being* finds its source in
God. *I am black because God is black!* God as creator
means that he is the ground of my blackness (being),

[18] Kaufmann, *op. cit.*, p. 140.

the point of reference for meaning and purpose in the universe.

If God, and not white people, is the ground of my being, then he is the only source for reference regarding how I should behave in the world. Complete obedience belongs only to him, and every alien loyalty must be rejected. Therefore, as a black man living in a white world that defines human existence according to white inhumanity, I cannot relax and pretend that all is well with black people. Rather it is incumbent upon me by the freedom granted in the creator himself to deny whiteness and affirm blackness as the essence of God. That is why it is necessary to speak of the Black Revolution rather than reformation. The idea of reformation suggests that there is still something "good" in the system itself, which needs only to be cleaned up a bit. This is a false perception of reality. The system is based on whiteness, and what is necessary is a replacement of whiteness with blackness. God as creator means that oppressed man is free to revolutionize the society, assured that his acts of liberation are the work of God himself.

2. *Immanence and Transcendence of God.* The immanence of God means that God always encounters us in a situation of historical liberation. That is why Christianity is called a historical religion. God is not a symbol referring to man's inward religious experiences, and neither is he a God of the Deist philosophers, who pictured God as performing the initial act of creation

but refraining from any further involvement in the world. According to biblical religion, God is involved in the concrete affairs of human history, liberating men from oppression. Therefore to ask, "Who is God?" is to focus on what he is doing; and to look at what he is doing is to center on human events as they pertain to the liberation of suffering humanity.

God then is not that pious feeling in our hearts and neither is he a being "out there" or "up there." It is not possible to speak of the reality of the divine in scientific categories. Like the symbol transcendence, immanence is not a causal term. It refers to the depths of liberation in human society, affirming that God is never less than our experience of liberation. The immanence of God is the infinite expressing himself in the finite. It is God becoming concrete in finite human existence. Man is able to speak of the divine because the divine is revealed in the concreteness of his world. The immanence of God then forces man to look for God in the world and to make decisions about the Ultimate in terms of present historical reality. Man cannot postpone his decision about God or condition it in terms of a future reality. The finality of God is his involvement in man's now-experiences. For black people this means that God has taken on blackness, involving himself in the dimensions of the black liberation struggle.

Though Black Theology stresses the immanence of God, it does not deny the reality of his transcendence. The transcendence of God prevents us from deifying our own experiences, which results in pantheism. God is not nature and neither is he our highest aspirations. God is always more than our experience of him. This means that truth is not limited to man's own capabilities. It is this reality that frees the rebel to give all for the liberation struggle without having to worry about the Western concept of winning. When black people say then that "all is in God's hand," this should not be equated with the trite expression "We should do nothing." It should be taken to mean that black people are now free to be for the black community, to make decisions about their existence in the world without an undue preoccupation with white ideas about "odds" (we have all the guns) or victory (you cannot win). Ultimately (and this is what God's transcendence means) black humanity is not dependent on our power to win. Despite the empirical odds, our involvement in our liberation is not pointless; it is not absurd. It refers to the depth and meaning of our being-in-the-world.

It is interesting that, though white "Christians" say they adhere to the meaning of Christ's existence in the world, they are especially concerned about "winning." The military budget of this country is evidence of this fact. When confronted with the uncompromising demands of the black community, they quickly remind us that they have all of the guns, as if that fact itself is supposed to make black people stay in their place. Being "Christian," they should know that Jesus was crucified because he did not stay in his place. In fact, that is what authentic Christian existence is all about, *the refusal to stay in one's place*. Of course, this may mean physical death, but death is beside the point when one knows that there is a depth to existence that transcends death. The death and resurrection of Christ expressed God's transcendence; that is, man does not have to live on the basis of mere physical existence. He is free to transcend it, free to encounter the presence of the infinite which transcends physical reality. This is why black people do not have to cling to physical life as if it is the ultimate.

Like immanence, transcendence is not a spatial concept. God is not "above" or "beyond" the world. Rather transcendence refers to man's purpose as defined by the infinite in the struggle for liberation. For black people, this means that their humanity is not defined by sociological reports and scientific studies. There is a transcendent value in blackness that makes us all human and to which black people must appeal as ultimate. Human dignity transcends human calculation. White people try to tell black people what is "best" for them in scientific terms as if blackness is subject to white measurements. But to white people's surprise, blacks reject their definitions, because black people know that they are not things to be computerized and limited according to white tools. We are *free*, free to defy the oppressor's laws of human behavior because we have encountered the concreteness of the divine in our liberation which revealed to us the transcendence of our cause beyond all human definitions.

The tension between the transcendence and immanence of God is what Paul Tillich calls the risk of faith. To speak of God is to speak, on the one hand, of the presence of the infinite in the finite concrete world. On the other hand, the infinite can never be reduced to the finite. Though the infinite is not equated with finite existence, yet because man can only encounter the infinite in his own finiteness, he must speak of the finite as if it is the ultimate. Tillich calls this "the infinite tension between the absoluteness of its claim and the relativity of its life." [19] Relating this to black people, Black Theology interprets this to mean our struggle for liberation is the infinite participating in the concrete reality of human existence. But because God is more than our experience of him, his reality is never limited to a particular human experience. However, just because God is more than black people's encounter of him in a particular moment of liberation, this should not be interpreted to mean that we must qualify our assertions about him. Just the opposite. Because God is not less than our experience of him, we must speak with an absoluteness that does not compromise with evil, despite the relativity of our claims.

3. *Providence.* It is difficult to talk about divine providence while men are dying and children are tortured. Richard Rubenstein pointed out the dangers of this concept in his excellent book entitled *After Auschwitz.*[20] Whether or not we agree with his conclusion

[19] Tillich, *Dynamics of Faith*, p. 57.
[20] New York: Bobbs-Merrill Co., 1966.

about the death of God, we can appreciate his analysis, since it is based on his identification with an oppressed people. Like Black Theology, Rubenstein refuses to affirm any view of God which contributes to the oppression of the Jewish people. If God is the Lord of history directing the course of events toward a final goal, and if the Jews are his elected people, then there is no way to avoid divine responsibility for the death of six million Jews in Germany, according to Rubenstein. Therefore, rather than accept a view of God that uses Jewish blood in his divine plan, he concludes that God is dead. The argument is cogent and certainly advances the death-of-God theology beyond white Christian views as represented in the thinking of William Hamilton and Thomas Altizer.

Rubenstein was not the first to recognize the difficulty of reconciling human suffering and divine participation in history. Without focusing on the God of history, the writer of Job recognized this problem; and in recent writing Albert Camus and the existentialists have dealt with it also. In Camus's thinking, if God is omnipotent and permits human suffering, then he is a murderer. That is why he quotes Bakunin with approval: "If God did exist, we would have to abolish Him."

Traditional Christian theology somehow fails to take this problem seriously. While intellectually giving credence to human suffering as a reality which appears to conflict with God's love, theologians still insist on quoting Paul with approval: "We know that in everything God works for good with those who love him, who are called according to his purpose" (Romans 8:28). Emil Brunner's view of divine providence is perhaps representative. He begins by distinguishing between God as creator and his providential care of the world. Avoiding both pantheism and deism, he writes:

> There is an existence which is not that of God, but is a creaturely existence, one therefore which is distinguished from the existence of God. Without a certain independent existence the creature cannot stand over against God, and if it does not do so, then it is not a creature as contrasted with the Creator. Even if we do not speak of a *creatio continuo* we imply that even now God does not cease to create an existence distinct from His own, a manner of existence which is different from His. If this be so, then there is also an activity of God in and on this existence which is distinct from himself, in and on the world He has created, which is not the activity of the Creator, but of the Preserver, the Ruler. . . .[21]

After describing providence as a distinguishable activity of God from his activity as creator, Brunner proceeds to define the meaning of divine providence. Providence, he says, means that "all that is, and all that happens, takes place within the knowledge and the will of God." There is nothing that happens that does not fit into God's ultimate plan for man. "All that hap-

[21] Brunner, *The Christian Doctrine of Creation and Redemption*, trans. by Olive Wyon (Philadelphia: The Westminster Press, 1952), p. 149.

pens is connected with the divine Purpose; all is ordered in accordance with, and in subordination to, the divine plan and the final divine purpose." [22]

If providence means what Brunner says, it is difficult, if not impossible, to avoid the conclusion that all human suffering is in accordance with divine plan. This would mean that the death of six million Jews, the genocide of the American Indian, the enslavement and lynching of black people, and every other inhumanity happened "within the knowledge and will of God." Only oppressors are able to make this claim. Of course, my opponents could reply that this view of providence does not mean that God *wills* human suffering. It simply means that he permits it in order to protect human freedom. It means further that, though man oppresses his brother, God will not let man have the last word about human existence, but translates man's evil into the divine purpose. Quoting Paul with approval, Brunner says, "I reckon that the sufferings of this present time are not worthy to be compared with the glory which shall be revealed to us-ward" (Romans 8:18). The believer looks beyond his suffering to the final goal which it must serve; compared with that promised glory, his suffering does not count. Suffering becomes the way to eternal life. No human suffering is overlooked by God, and thus providence means that it is redeemable. Thus "the real solution to the problem of theodicy is redemption." [23]

[22] *Ibid.*, p. 155.
[23] *Ibid.*, p. 183.

Despite the emphasis on future redemption in present suffering, Black Theology cannot accept any view
of God that even *indirectly* places divine approval on
human suffering. The death and resurrection of Christ
does not mean that God promises us a future reality in
order that we might bear the present evil. The suffering that Christ accepted and which is promised to his
disciples is not to be equated with the easy acceptance
of human injustice inflicted by white oppressors. God
cannot be the God of black people and also will their
suffering. To be elected by God does not mean freely
accepting the evils of the oppressors; but the suffering
which is inseparable from the gospel is that style of existence that arises from a decision to *be* in spite of
nonbeing. It is that type of suffering that is inseparable
from freedom, that freedom that affirms black liberation despite the white powers of evil. It is suffering in
the struggle for liberation.

Providence then is not a statement about the future.
It does not mean that all things will work out for the
best for those who love God. Providence is a statement
about present reality—the reality of the liberation of
the oppressed. For black people, it is a statement about
the reality of blackness and what it means in the liberation struggle against white people. As Tillich says,
"Faith in providence is faith 'in spite of—in spite of the
. . . meaninglessness of existence." [24] Again speaking of
special providence, he writes, it "gives the individual
the certainty that under any circumstances, under any

[24] Tillich, *Systematic Theology*, Vol. I, p. 264.

set of conditions, the divine 'factor' is active and that therefore the road to his ultimate fulfillment is open." [25] Black Theology interprets this to mean that in spite of whiteness a way is open to blackness, and we do not have to accept white definitions.

It is within this context that divine omnipotence should be interpreted. Omnipotence does not refer to God's absolute power to accomplish what he wants. But as John Macquarrie says, omnipotence is "the power to let something stand out from nothing and to be." [26] Translating this idea into the black experience, God's omnipotence is the power to let black people stand out from whiteness and to be. It is what happens when black people make ready for the black-white encounter with the full determination that they shall have their freedom or else. In this situation, divine providence is seeing divine reality in the present reality of black liberation, no more and no less.

[25] *Ibid.*, p. 267.
[26] Macquarrie, *God and Secularity* (Philadelphia: The Westminster Press, 1967), p. 123.

V

Man in Black Theology

Although Christian theology is essentially God-talk, we must not forget who it is that speaks of God. The finiteness of man means that we cannot transcend human existence even when we speak of the transcendent God. We know who God is not because we can move beyond our finiteness but because the transcendent God has become immanent in our history, transforming human events into divine events of liberation. It is the *divine* involvement in historical events of liberation that makes theology God-centered; but because God participates in man's historical liberation, we can only speak of God as he is related to man. In this sense, theology is anthropology. In order to clarify the black perspective on theological anthropology, it will be useful to compare it with certain examples of American theology and of existential philosophy.

American Theology, Existentialism, and Black Theology

The weakness of most "Christian" approaches to man stems from a preoccupation with (and distortion of) the God-problem, leaving concrete, oppressed man unrecognized and degraded. This is evident, for instance, in fundamentalist and orthodox theologies when they view the infallibility of the Bible as the sole ground of religious authority and fail to ask about the relevance of the inerrancy of Scripture to the wretched of the earth. If the basic truth of the gospel is that the Bible is the infallible Word of God, then it is inevitable that more emphasis will be placed upon "true" propositions about God than upon God as he is active in the liberation of the oppressed of the land. Black people, struggling for survival, are not interested in the abstract truth, "infallible" or otherwise. Truth is concrete.

The same God-emphasis is evident among American Barthians, who talk about the absolute sovereignty of God in his self-revelation, but say nothing about God's revelation as he is related to blacks who are forced to live in rat-infested ghettos. These theologians are silent on the real human issues. It may be interesting in a seminary class to talk about God's self-disclosure and how this view of revelation renders the traditional proofs of God's existence invalid. But most black people never heard of Aristotle, Anselm, Descartes, or Kant, and they do not care about the relationship of theology and philosophy. Unless God's revelation is related to black liberation, then black people must reject it. The Barthians have confused God-talk with white-talk, and thus have failed to see that there is no real speech about God except as he is participating in the liberation of the oppressed.

Unfortunately the liberal theologians have been guilty of the same error. Though they may have stressed God's love and neighborly love in human relations, it was done with a white emphasis. They stressed God's love at the expense of black liberation, failing to articulate the right of black people to defend themselves against white racists. They asked black people to turn the other cheek (so they could be "like" Jesus) while white people were destroying them. It is true that some liberals "helped" black people by persuading white people to be nice to us, and this probably prevented some lynchings. But black people know that a person can be lynched in other ways than hanging him from a tree. What about depriving him of his humanity by suggesting that white humanity is man as God intended him to be? What about the liberal emphasis on the goodness of man at the same time white people were doing everything they could to destroy black people?

It is disappointing, though perhaps understandable, that the death-of-God theology and secular theologies are following the same pattern. They ask us to embrace humanity and its urban manifestation, but fail miserably in relating this "new humanism" to the inhumanity committed against black people. "God is dead," they tell us, but black people are not impressed because we know that this is the white attempt to make life meaningful for white people in spite of their brutality to the black community.

Because Black Theology begins with the black condition as the fundamental datum of human experience, we cannot gloss over the importance of man and the concreteness of human oppression in the world in which black people are condemned to live. In this concern for the concreteness of man, Black Theology resembles existentialism, with its conviction that "existence precedes essence" (to use Sartre's phrase). This means that concrete man must be the point of departure of any phenomenological analysis of human existence. According to Sartre, there is no essence or universal humanity independent of man in the concreteness of his involvement in the world. Each man defines his own essence by participating in the world, making decisions that involve himself and all men.

Sartre's emphasis on man's concreteness and the awesome responsibility of making decisions that include all men has led him to deny the reality of God. To speak of the freedom of man necessarily means the exclusion not only of God but also of every appeal to a common human nature. Sartre's humanism excludes God and universals because they enslave human beings and deprive them of the possibilities inherent in the future.[1]

Unlike Sartre, Camus (who refused to refer to himself as an existentialist) appeals to a common value among men which is capable of recognition by all and which is responsible for man's revolt against human oppression. The affirmation of a common value accounts for Camus's popularity among religionists. He appears to leave open the question of God. That, however, was not his intention, since (like Sartre) he denies the relevance of God to man's existence. The experience of the absurd as disclosed in the reality of human suffering cannot be reconciled with belief in an omnipotent God.[2]

Black Theology, while declining to enter the debate on human nature between Camus and Sartre, concurs in the intensity with which they focus on oppressed men. And although we see no need to deny the existence of God, we are glad for the presence of Camus and Sartre to remind theologians that the God-problem must never be permitted to detract from the concern for real man. The sole purpose of God in Black Theol-

[1] For an introduction to Sartre's perspective, see his *Existentialism and Human Emotions* (New York: Philosophical Library, 1957). His most detailed philosophical work is *Being and Nothingness*.

[2] For an introduction to Camus, see his *Myth of Sisyphus*, trans. by J. O'Brien (New York: Random House, 1955), and *The Rebel*.

ogy is to illuminate the black condition so that black
people can see that their liberation is the manifestation
of his activity. We believe then that we can learn more
about God, and therefore about man, by examining
black people as they get ready to do their thing than
by reading some erudite discourse on man by a white
theologian. God in Christ meets us in the situation of
our oppressed condition and tells us not only who *he* is
and what *he* is doing about our liberation, but also
who *we* are and what *we* must do about white people.
If black people can take Christology seriously, then it
follows that the meaning of our anthropology is also
found in and through our oppressed condition, as we
do what we have to about the presence of white people.

Some readers will object to the absence of the "universal note" in the foregoing assertions, asking, "How
can you reconcile the lack of universalism regarding
human nature with a universal God?" The first reply is
to deny that there is a "universal God" in the normal
understanding of the concept. As pointed out in the
previous chapter, God is black. Secondly, Black Theology is suspicious of people who appeal to a universal,
ideal humanity. The oppressors are ardent lovers of humanity. They can love all men in general, even black
people, because intellectually they can put black people in the category called Humanity. With this
perspective they can participate in civil rights and help
blacks purely on the premise that they are a part of the

ideal man. But when it comes to dealing with particular blacks, statistics transformed into black-encounter, they are at a loss. They remind us of Dostoevsky's doctor, who said, "I love humanity, but I wonder at myself. The more I love humanity in general, the less I love man in particular." [3]

The basic mistake of our white opponents is their failure to see that God did not become a universal man but an oppressed Jew, thereby disclosing to us that both man's nature and God's are inseparable from oppression and liberation. To know who man *is* is to focus on the Oppressed One and what he does for an oppressed community as they liberate themselves from slavery. Christ is not a man for all people; he is a man for oppressed people whose identity is made known in and through their liberation. Therefore our definition of man must be limited to what it means to be liberated from human oppression. Any other analysis fails to recognize the reality of suffering in an inhuman society. Black Theology cannot affirm a higher harmony of the universe which sidesteps the suffering of black people. We are reminded of Dostoevsky's Ivan Karamazov and his rejection of God because of the suffering of children.

I renounce the higher harmony altogether. It's not worth the tears of that one tortured child who beat itself on the

[3] Fyodor Dostoevsky, *The Brothers Karamazov*, trans. by Constance Garnett (New York: Modern Library, 1950), p. 64.

breast with its little fist and prayed in its stinking out-
house, with its unexpiated tears to "dear kind God!"

To experience the sufferings of little children is to reject universal man in favor of particular men. It forces
you to say something that takes seriously the meaning
of human suffering. White people can move beyond
particular man to universal man because they have not
experienced the reality of *color*. This is the meaning of
Maulana Ron Karenga's comment:

> Man is only man in a philosophy class or a biology lab.
> In the world he is African, Asian or South American. He
> is a Chinese making a cultural revolution, or an Afro-
> American with soul. He lives by bread and butter, enjoys
> red beans and rice, or watermelon and ice cream.[4]

The inability of American theology to define man in
the light of the Oppressed One and of particular oppressed people stems from its identity with the structures of white power. Man in American theology is
George Washington, Thomas Jefferson and Abraham
Lincoln rolled into one and polished up a bit. He is
colorless man, capable of "accepting" the black man as
his brother, which means that he does not mind the
black man living next door *if* he behaves himself. But it
is at this very point that American theology ceases to

[4] Quoted in Archie Hargraves, "The Meanings of Black Power,"
Register, The Chicago Theological Seminary, Vol. LIX, No. 2 (De-
cember, 1968), p. 31.

speak of man in any real sense. Actually, only the oppressed know what man is because they have encountered both the depravity of human behavior from the
oppressors and also the healing powers as revealed in
the Oppressed One. Having experienced the brutality
of human pride, they will speak less of man's goodness;
but also having encountered the meaning of liberation,
they can and must speak of human worth as revealed
in the black community itself affirming its blackness.

Since we have defined our point of departure as the
manifestation of the Oppressed One as he is involved
in the liberation of an oppressed community, it is now
appropriate to ask, "What is man?" That is, what is it
that makes man what he is, thereby distinguishing him
essentially from everything else that exists? [5] The question of man then is not a question of enumerating
properties; he is not a collection of properties that can
be scientifically analyzed. Rather to speak of man is to
speak about his being-in-the-world-of-human-oppres-
sion. With the reality of human suffering as our starting point, what can Black Theology say about man?

Man as a Free Being

1. Freedom as Liberation. If the content of the gospel
is liberation, the existence of man must be explained as

[5] See Gajo Petrović, *Marx in the Mid-Twentieth Century* (New
York: Doubleday and Co., 1967), p. 75.

"being in freedom," which means that he rebels against every form of slavery, the oppression of everything creative. "A slave," writes LeRoi Jones, "cannot be a man." [6] To be man is to be free, and to be free is to be man. The free man is the one who defines the meaning of his being in terms of the oppressed of the land by participating in their liberation, fighting against everything that is against man. Only the oppressed are truly free!

This is the paradox of human existence. *Freedom is the opposite of oppression, but only the oppressed are truly free.* How can this be? On the one hand, the concreteness of human existence reveals that man is not man when his creative expressions are enslaved by alien powers. To be man is to be separated from everything that is evil, everything that is against the "extension of the limits of humanity." [7] But on the other hand, human existence also discloses that the reality of evil is an ever-present possibility in our finite world, and to be man means to be identified with those who are enslaved as they fight against human evil. Being man is the same as being against evil by joining sides with those who are the victims of evil. Quite literally, it means becoming oppressed with the oppressed, making their cause our cause by involving ourselves in the liberation struggle. *No man is free until all men are free.*

---

[6] LeRoi Jones, *Blues People* (New York: William Morrow and Co., 1963), p. 60.

[7] Petrović, *op. cit.*, p. 127.

Paul Tillich expresses this paradox in his analysis of the relation between being and nonbeing. On the one hand, being is the opposite of nonbeing. To *be* is to participate in Being which is the source of everything that is. To exist is to exist in freedom, *i.e.*, stand out from nonbeing and *be*.[8] But, on the other hand, finite being "does not stand completely out of non-being."[9] Always there, is the threat of nothingness, the possibility of ceasing to be. Man, therefore, is a creature who seeks to be in spite of nonbeing. The power to be in spite of nonbeing is what Tillich call courage. "The courage to be is the ethical act in which man affirms his being in spite of those elements of his existence which conflict with essential self-affirmation."[10]

Inherent in freedom is the recognition that there is something wrong with the society, and one will not be content until all men are treated as persons. There comes a time in every man's life when he realizes that the world is not as he dreams, and he has to make a choice: submit or risk all.[11] Being free means that the only real choice is risking all. A man is prepared to risk all when he perceives the true nature of the society and what it means to oppressed people. When a man comes to this recognition, he also real-

[8] See Tillich, *Systematic Theology*, Vol. II, p. 20 ff.
[9] *Ibid.*, p. 20.
[10] Tillich, *The Courage to Be* (New Haven: Yale University Press, 1952), p. 3.
[11] See Ignazio Silone, *Bread and Wine*, trans. by Harvey Fergusson II (New York: A Signet Classic, 1963), p. 41 ff.

izes, as does Ignazio Silone's Pietro Spina in *Bread and Wine,* that freedom must be taken.

> Freedom is not something you get as a present. . . . You can live in a dictatorship and be free—on one condition: that you fight the dictatorship. The man who thinks with his own mind and keeps it uncorrupted is free. The man who fights for what he thinks is right is free. But you can live in the most democratic country on earth, and if you're lazy, obtuse or servile within yourself, you're not free. Even without any violent coercion, you're a slave. You can't beg your freedom from someone. You have to seize it—everyone as much as he can.[12]

It is not difficult for the oppressed to understand the meaning of freedom. They are forced by the very nature of their condition to interpret their existence in the world contrary to the value-structures of the oppressive society. For the oppressed, to be is to be in revolt against the forces that impede the creation of the new man. This is what Karl Marx has in mind in his definition of man as praxis which means "directed activity." [13] Praxis expresses man's freedom. "Freedom," writes Marx, "is the essence of man." [14] It "*is not something outside one who freely is, it is the specific mode or structure of being*," [15] and inherent in it is ac-

[12] *Ibid.,* p. 43.
[13] See Norman A. Bailey, "Toward a Praxeological Theory of Conflict," *Orbis,* Vol. XI, No. 4 (Winter, 1968), pp. 1081–1112.
[14] Quoted in Jacques Maritain, *Moral Philosophy,* trans. by Marshall Suther (New York: Charles Scribner's Sons, 1964), p. 236.
[15] Petrović, *op. cit.,* p. 122. Petrovic's italics.

tion. Marx says: "The coincidence of the changing circumstances and of human activity can be conceived and rationally understood only as revolutionizing practice (praxis)." [16] Here he shows the inseparable relationship of freedom and liberation activity. To be man is to be involved, participating in the societal structures for human liberation. As Petrović puts it: "*The question of the essence of freedom,* like the question of the essence of man, *is not only a question.* It is *at once participation in production of freedom.* It is an activity through which freedom frees itself." [17]

Freedom then is not an abstract question. It deals with human existence in a world of societal enslavement. We cannot solve the question of freedom in a college classroom, theoretically debating the idea of "freedom versus determinism." Freedom is an existential reality. It is not a question about rational thought but human confrontation. It is not solved by academic discussion but risky human encounter. As Silone's Spina says, "Man doesn't really exist unless he's fighting against his own limits." [18]

To be free means that man is not an object, and he will not let others treat him as an it. He refuses to let limits be put on his being. He is at once a part of nature (subject to laws of the universe) and is indepen-

[16] Karl Marx, "Theses on Feuerbach," in Lewis S. Feuer, ed., *Marx and Engels: Basic Writings on Politics and Philosophy* (Garden City: Doubleday and Co., 1959), p. 244.
[17] Petrović, *op. cit.,* p. 120. Petrovic's italics.
[18] Silone, *op. cit.,* p. 179.

dent of nature. Dostoevsky makes this point in the *Notes from Underground:* "Great Heavens, what are the laws of nature to me! . . . Obviously I cannot pierce this wall with my forehead . . . but neither will I reconcile myself to it just because it is a stone wall." Or again, he writes: "The whole human enterprise consists exclusively in man proving to himself every moment that he is man and not a cog." People who insist on treating human beings as cogs must be made to realize that man is not a robot but is a free, living organism, capable of making the most of human creativity. Liberation is nothing but a putting into practice the reality of human freedom.

2. *Freedom and the Image of God.* The being of man as freedom is expressed in the Bible in terms of the image of God. Even though there has been much talk about the *imago Dei* in the history of theology, most religionists have not given proper attention to the concept of existential freedom and its relation to the image of God. Theologians seem to have a way of making simple ideas obscure by the way they spend their energies debating fine points. (It is little wonder that nonprofessionals think that theology is unrelated to man's ordinary involvement in the world.)

In the history of theology, the image of God is generally conceived of as man's *rationality* and *freedom*.[19]

---

[19] See H. Wheeler Robinson, *The Christian Doctrine of Man* (Edinburgh: T. & T. Clark, 1958), and David Cairns, *The Image of God in Man* (London: Lutterworth Press, 1939), for an account of how men have thought about this idea.

Justin's statement is representative of the Patristic period: "In the beginning He made the human race with the power of thought and of choosing the truth and doing right, so that all men are without excuse before God; for they have been born rational and contemplative." [20] It is significant that freedom and rational reflection go hand in hand, without any connection to the rebellion of the oppressed. Medieval thought was similarly defective, as the image was interpreted in terms of an *analogia entis,* which means that man's being as such is in the likeness of the being of God.

The Reformation reinterpreted the image to include the personal encounter between God and man and deemphasized man's rational ability to know God. Luther even speaks of reason as a "whore" that deceives man by causing the creature to think that he is God. To say that man was created in the image of God, for Luther, meant that "man was in a relation to God that was wholly based on and governed by God's grace, to which man responded with faith." [21] It was the kind of relationship which is analogous to a child's relationship to his father. Just as the child responds to his father in obedience and trust, man in the image of God responds to God with trustful obedience. Commenting on Luther's view of man's original righteousness (image of God) P. S. Watson says:

[20] Robinson, *op. cit.,* p. 164.
[21] P. S. Watson, *The Concept of Grace* (Philadelphia: Muhlenberg Press, 1959), p. 82.

It was a state in which his whole life was so centered in God, that in thought, will and action he was governed solely by the good and gracious will of God. It was as if he had "no will of his own," no desire but to do the will of God, whose word of command and promise he implicitly believed. That was what constituted man's "original righteousness"—the right relationship to God, and therefore to all else, for which and in which he was created.[22]

It is to Luther's credit that he added the personal dimension in contrast to the rationalistic approach of medieval theology. But it is to his discredit that he failed to relate this concept to the social and political conditions of the oppressed. Luther's identification with the structures of power weakened his view of the image of God. The idea that man is free to challenge the state with force when it oppresses men is not present in his thinking.

Modern theology, following Schleiermacher's unhappy clue to the relationship of theology and anthropology, forgot about Luther's emphasis on the depravity of man and proceeded once again to make appeals to man's goodness. The nineteenth century is known for its confidence in rational man, who not only knew what was right but was capable of responding to it. The image of God in man was the guarantee that the world was moving in a desirable direction. Of course, it never occurred to our "Christian" thinkers that they had missed some contrary evidence, since this was the

[22] Ibid., p. 82.

period of black enslavement and Indian extermination, as well as of European conquests in Africa and Asia.

World War I did much to shatter this ungodly view of man. Karl Barth with his *Epistle to the Romans* commentary, Rudolf Bultmann with his existential, form-critical approach, Paul Tillich with his ontology, Emil Brunner with his own brand of neo-orthodoxy, and Reinhold Niebuhr with his ethical orientation made such an impact on liberalism that we are likely never to see it again the way it used to be. These men did not share liberalism's confidence in man; like the reformers, they emphasized man's depravity, the inability of the creature to transcend finite existence. The image of God in man is not to be identified with abstract rationality or freedom. Although all the so-called neo-orthodox theologians had unique approaches to the idea of the image, they all agreed that it involved the whole person in a divine-human encounter. Refuting the Thomistic concept of an *analogia entis,* Bonhoeffer says:

> There is no analogy between God and man, if only because God—the only One existing in and for himself in his underived being, yet at the same time existing for his creatures, binding and giving his freedom to man—must not be thought of as being alone; in-as-much as he is the God who in Christ bears witness to his "being for man." [23]

[23] Bonhoeffer, *Creation and Fall,* trans. by John Fletcher (New York: The Macmillan Co., 1959), pp. 36-37.

Bonhoeffer prefers to speak of an *analogia relationis* which is not a part of man, not a structure of his being, and neither is it a capacity. It is a given relationship in which man is free to be for God because God is free for him in Christ.

> The analogy, the likeness must be understood strictly as follows: the likeness has its likeness *only* from the original. It always refers us only to the original, and is "like" only in this way. *Analogia relationis* is therefore the relation given by God. . . . The relation of creature with creature is a God-given relation because it exists in freedom and freedom originates from God.[24]

Black Theology can appreciate the new emphasis, but it is not enough to identify the image with *analogia relationis,* as Bonhoeffer himself apparently realized later when Hitler's pretensions to deity became evident. If the image of God includes freedom, as is definitely implied in the divine-human encounter, then it must also include *liberation.* Even though Karl Barth was opposed to them, the liberals were right in their stress on freedom as an essential element of the *imago Dei,* though they had the wrong idea of freedom. Freedom is not a rational decision about possible alternatives; it is a participation of the whole man in the liberation struggle. The Barthians were right on the personal aspect of freedom in the divine-human en-

[24] *Ibid.,* p. 37.

counter, but they failed to place due emphasis on the role of liberation in an oppressive society.

The biblical concept of image means that man is created in such a way that he cannot obey oppressive laws and still be man. To be man is to be in the image of God, *i.e.*, to be creative—revolting against everything that is against man. Therefore, whatever we say about sin and man's inability to know God because of the Fall, it must not in any way diminish the freedom of man to be in revolt against his oppressors. As Gerhard Von Rad says: "The Priestly account of man's creation . . . speaks less of the nature of God's image than of its purpose. There is less said about the gift itself than about the task." Man's task, according to Von Rad, is the "domination in the world, especially over the animals." [25] In view of the Exodus we must also say that the task includes a participation in the freedom of God in the liberation of his people. Jürgen Moltmann puts it this way: "Jahweh is . . . the God who leads his people out of the house of bondage. Thus he is a God of freedom, the God ahead of us. One acquires social, political, and world-surpassing freedom from God, not against him." [26]

It is the biblical concept of the image of God that makes black rebellion in America human. When black

[25] Gerhard Von Rad, *Genesis*, trans. by John Marks (Philadelphia: The Westminster Press, 1961), p. 57.

[26] Jürgen Moltmann, "The Revolution of Freedom: The Christian and Marxist Struggle" in Thomas Ogletree, ed., *Openings for Marxist Christian Dialogue* (Nashville: Abingdon Press, 1968), p. 53.

people affirm their freedom in God, they must say No to white people. By saying No, they say Yes to God, to their blackness, affirming at the same time the inhumanity of the white neighbor who insists on being God. Black Theology then emphasizes the right of black people to be black and by so doing to participate in the image of God.

The image of God refers to the way in which God intends for man to live in the world. The image of God is thus more than rationality, more than what so-called neoorthodox theologians call divine-human encounter. In a world in which men are oppressed, the image is man in rebellion against the structures of oppression. It is man involved in the liberation struggle against the forces of inhumanity.

3. *Freedom as Identification with an Oppressed Community.* It is important to point out that freedom is not white middle-class individualism. It has nothing to do with reading and writing poetry or joining Students for a Democratic Society. It is not to be equated with Hippies or Yippies—the long hair and all that jazz. This is not intended as a put-down of white young people who are moving against their elders for one of the first times in American history; and we should say that they do appear to be quite human at times. The positive value of these "unusual" manifestations is their seeming recognition that there is something wrong with killing people in Vietnam and with the oppression of people generally—contrary to the

long-standing assumptions of this society. The beginning of freedom is the perception that oppressors are
the evil ones, and that we must do something about it.

But the truly free man takes one more step. He
also recognizes that freedom becomes a reality when
he throws in his lot with the cause of the oppressed
community by joining with them in their cause, accepting whatever is necessary to be identified with the
victims of evil. The problem of many white groups is
becoming truly identified with the black community.
Like their elders, they seem to expect black people
to accept them without too much emotional feeling
about the past. When black people reject them, they
quickly turn in on themselves, forming their own esoteric little groups, saying, "Blacks want in and we are
trying to get out."

To be free is to participate in a community of those
who are victims of oppression. Man is free when he belongs to a free community seeking to emancipate itself
from oppression. Freedom then is more than just making decisions in the light of one's individual taste during moments of existence. It always involves making
decisions within the context of a community of people
who share similar goals and are seeking the same liberation. Freedom means taking sides in a crisis situation
when a society is divided between oppressed and oppressors. In this situation we are not permitted the luxury of being on neither side by making a decision that
only involves the self. Our decision involves all men,

and it must be made in view of either the oppressed or the oppressor. There is no way to transcend this alternative. The truly free man is identified with the humiliated because he knows that his own being is involved in his brother's degradation. He cannot stand to see his brother stripped of his humanity. This is so not because of his pity or sympathy, but because his own existence is being limited by another's slavery. He does not need to ask whether his brother is at fault. All he knows is that there is a fight going on, and he must choose sides, without any assurance of who is right in the "Christian" sense of future victory for the oppressed. Mathieu, the protagonist in Sartre's *The Age of Reason,* recognized the difficulty of being truly free by renouncing a false freedom. Thinking to himself during his encounter with Brunet, who was trying to persuade him to join the party, he says:

"At this moment, at this very moment, there are men firing point-blank at one another in the suburbs of Madrid, there are Austrian Jews agonizing in concentration camps, there are Chinese burning under the ruins of Nanking, and here I am, in perfect health, I feel quite free, in a quarter of an hour I shall take my hat and go for a walk in the Luxembourg." He turned towards Brunet and looked at him with bitterness. "I am one of the *irresponsibles*," he thought.[27]

[27] Sartre, *The Age of Reason,* trans. by Eric Sutton (New York: Bantam Books, 1968), p. 133.

Freedom is more than intellectual articulation of an existential philosophical attitude. It involves the commitment of one's whole being for the cause of the oppressed. That is why Brunet says:

"You're all the same, you intellectuals: everything is cracking and collapsing, the guns are on the point of going off, and you stand there calmly claiming the right to be convinced. If only you could see yourselves with my eyes, you would understand that time presses." [28]

But that is just the point; the oppressor can never see himself as the oppressed see him. Brunet is wasting his time. If men always have to be *told* about the inhumanity around them, there is little hope for man. Even Mathieu knows intellectually that Brunet is right and that he ought to make a choice. At one moment he says to himself regarding Brunet: "He is freer than I: he is in harmony with himself and with the party." [29]

In order to be free, a man must be able to make choices that are not dependent on the oppressive system. Mathieu is able to live an irresponsible life that some might call "freedom" because he participates in a society that protects him. He is insensitive to the suffering of others, even that of his own mistress, Marcelle. If he cannot choose a freedom that involves his intimate friend, it is not likely that he will be able to

[28] *Ibid.*, p. 134.
[29] *Ibid.*, p. 133.

choose a freedom that involves unknown sufferers. As Sartre says: "The only way of helping the enslaved out there is to take sides with those who are here."

It seems that this is the major weakness of white people who say that they are concerned about humanity. With all due respect to white concern for the war in Vietnam, the authenticity of the response must be questioned. The destruction of black humanity began long before the Vietnam war and few white people got upset about it. It is therefore appropriate to ask, "Is it because white boys are dying in the war that whites get so upset? Can we expect them to be equally involved in the destruction of their racism when the war is over? In view of their lack of concern for the oppression of black people before and during this ungodly massacre of Vietnam, is it likely that whites will turn their energies toward the oppressed in America?" If the past and present attitudes of whites are clues, we can expect that after the war has ceased and the troops are withdrawn, white America will be free to deal with the "black problem" the same way it always deals with any problem: Declare to black people what is required for them to exist, for their presence, and then proceed to destroy everyone who thinks otherwise.

It is an interesting work of logic that white religionists can get so perturbed about the Vietnam war but are not particularly concerned about black people. In regard to the oppression of black people, they can always make excuses and even suggest that black suffering is not too severe. The only way I can understand this logic is to see it for what it is—the logic of oppressors. Being white, it is only natural that their taste for humanity will arouse their sensitivities when they watch white boys leave for the war and come back in boxes. No one likes to see any member of *his community* destroyed. And in all likelihood, we can believe the President when he says that everything is being done to end the war, except pulling out all the troops. And even in that regard, they will be pulled out only when white "integrity" is preserved.

While the whiteness of white people enhances their protest against the war, it only increases their own determination to keep black people down. Being white excludes them from the black community and thus all their concern for black people will invariably work against black freedom. What whites fail to recognize is the fact that all decisions people make regarding what is important or worthwhile are made in the context of their participation in a community. It is in the community where values are chosen, because the community provides the structure in which our being as persons is realized. It is not possible to transcend the community; it decides our being because being is always *being in relation to others.*

But is it possible to change communities? To change communities involves a change of being. It is a radical movement, a radical reorientation of one's existence in the world. Christianity calls this experience conversion.

Certainly if white people expect to be able to say any-thing relevant to the self-determination of the black community, it will be necessary for them to destroy their whiteness by becoming members of an oppressed community. Whites will be free only when they be-come new persons—when their white being has passed away and they are created anew in black being. When this happens, they are no longer white but free and thus capable of making decisions about the destiny of the black community.

4. Freedom and Suffering. Since being free means participating in the liberation of an oppressed commu-nity, freedom is inevitably associated with suffering. Socially and existentially the free man will count his losses.

To assert one's freedom always involves encounter-ing the economic and social structures of oppression. When the rulers first perceive that one is a menace to the society, their initial response is to try to silence the undesirable by cutting off the sources of physical exis-tence and social involvement. This is to remind the rebel who's boss. The oppressors hope that by making it difficult to live, the rebel will come around to seeing the world the way the rulers view it. Coupled with economic oppression is social ostracism. The intention is to demonstrate the perversity of the rebel's involve-ment by picturing him as the destroyer of the "good." At no time is the rebel given the opportunity to define his way of looking at the world, because the mass media belong to the oppressors who will not permit the seditious presence to extend itself.

If economic and social oppression fail to bring the rebel into line, the structures of power begin to devise political means of silencing him. The rebel knows this because liberation always involves fighting against the powers that be, and they never take kindly to that. To go against the "keepers of peace" is to take a political risk, the risk of being shot, imprisoned, or exiled. That is why Silone's Spina says, "Freedom is not something you get as a present. . . . You can't beg your freedom from someone. You have to seize it—everyone as much as he can." Reinhold Niebuhr also made this point convincingly in *Moral Man and Immoral Society*, observing that people in power will never admit that the society rewards them far more than necessary considering the services rendered; and this attitude inevitably makes them enslave all who question their interests. The appeal to reason and religion do not change the balance of power because both are used to defend the interests of the oppressors. Change will take place, according to Niebuhr, when the enslaved recognize that power must be met with power. The black community is aware of this; and the black revolution is nothing but a will to spread the decision among black people to seize their freedom—any way they can. No black man will ever be good enough in the eyes of white people to merit equality. Therefore, if black people are to have freedom, we must take it, with guns if need be. For we now know as even Sartre's Mathieu recognized: "No one can be a man who has not discovered something for which he is prepared to die." [30]

Without minimizing the horror of social, economic, and political losses, it may at least be noted that these are expected by the oppressed, and that one's life can be adjusted to accommodate physical pain. It is not possible to be black and not know what white people do to black people. The presence of the black ghettos in every city where blacks live is a visible manifestation of white cruelty. But existential suffering is not easily recognized or readily dealt with. It refers to the pain associated with the absurdity of being black in a white racist world and with the responsibility of doing something about it. Growing up in America is an absurd experience for black people. At first, one does not know what is going on. He cannot figure out what he has done to merit the treatment accorded him. But then he realizes that white brutality is not related to his particular actions. It is white society's way of telling the black man that he is not a person. Now he must make a decision: either accept his place or resolve to call down upon himself the nothingness of white existence by revolting against the world as it is.

It is important to note that the absurdity arises not from the black man's perception of himself, but only from the attempt to reconcile his being with the white world. It is analogous to Albert Camus's philosophical

[30] *Ibid.*, p. 135.

analysis of absurdity. The absurd is the "strangeness of the world" when man tries to make sense out of it in relation to his existence. The absurd, writes Camus, is "the confrontation of this irrational and wild longing for clarity whose call echoes in the human heart." [31] There is suffering because there is no *hope* that the reconciliation will be possible, and the only authentic response is to face the reality of the absurdity in rebellion.

In another context, Sartre describes freedom in terms of anguish, forlornness, and despair. The three together point to the suffering which is inseparable from man's being-in-the-world. Anguish is the recognition that one's actions involve all men. "Man is anguish," writes Sartre, in that he is a creature capable of involvement, realizing that it is not possible to accept responsibility for all and not have some anxiety about it. We are thrown into the world with a multiplicity of possibilities but with no guide for correctness in choice. But whatever choice we make, it is not just our choice; it is a choice for all men. We assume the responsibility for humanity and declare what we consider to be the possibility of man. Who can make such a choice without feeling at the same time the deep sense of anxiety? This is the choice that every black man makes. He is alone and yet not alone, and there is no way to evade the seriousness of his responsibility.

Forlornness, writes Sartre, means that "God does not

[31] Camus, *The Myth of Sisyphus*, p. 16.

exist and that we have to face all the consequences of this." [32] The purpose is to deny "values in heaven" or an "*a priori* good." It is taking Dostoevsky seriously, "If God didn't exist, everything would be possible." Man knows that that is his situation, "and as a result man is forlorn, because neither within him nor without does he find anything to cling to." [33] He has no universal ethics to guide his existence in the world, and thus he is condemned to make his choices without any assurances. He chooses his existence.

Sartre's analysis of forlornness is especially appropriate for the oppressed. Oppression means that the society has defined truth in terms of human slavery; and liberation means the denial of that truth. The God of the society must be destroyed so that the oppressed can define existence in accordance with their liberation. In the moment of liberation, there are no universal truths; there is only the truth of liberation itself, which the oppressed themselves define in the struggle for freedom. To be forlorn is to accept the task of choosing humanity without any certainty beyond the existing moment.

It is not possible to experience oppression without also experiencing despair. Despair means that "we shall confine ourselves to reckoning only with what depends upon our will, or on the ensemble of probabilities which make our action possible." [34] We cannot move

[32] Sartre, *The Philosophy of Existentialism,* Wade Baskin, ed. (New York: Philosophical Library, 1965), pp. 45-46.

[33] *Ibid.,* p. 41.

[34] *Ibid.,* p. 45-46.

beyond our earthly possibilities. Again in Sartre's words, "I am left in the realm of possibility; but possibilities are to be reckoned with only to the point where my action comports with the ensemble of these possibilities and no further." [35] It is illegitimate to point to the *future* unless the pointing includes the recognition that "I am my future." To avoid this dimension of existence is to move to a false security. It is necessary for the oppressed to carve out the meaning of existence without appealing to alien values.

The relationship between freedom and suffering is also evident in the biblical tradition. The election of Israel is a call to share in Yahweh's liberation. It is not a position of privilege but of terrible responsibility. To be Yahweh's people, Israel must be willing to fight against everything that is against this liberation. Therefore, the whole of her history is a description of the movement of this people in relation to God's liberating work. This involves suffering because liberation means a confrontation between evil and the will of him who directs history.

The existence of Jesus Christ also discloses that freedom is bound up with suffering. It is not possible to be for him and not realize that one has chosen an existence in suffering. "Blessed are you when men revile you and persecute you . . . falsely on my account" (Matthew 5:11). The very character of human existence as defined in his life is enough to show that we cannot be for Jesus and for the societal humiliation of human

[35] *Ibid.,* p. 46.

beings. To be for him means being for the oppressed, as expressed in their self-determination. Jesus himself expresses this by limiting the Kingdom to the poor and unwanted. The Kingdom is for the poor because they represent the meaning of oppression and the certainty of liberation. Moltmann puts it well:

> If we believe the crucified Christ to be the representative of God on earth, we see the glory of God no longer in the crowns of the mighty but in the face of the man who was executed on the gallows. What the authorities intended to be the greatest humiliation—namely the cross—is thus transformed into the highest dignity. It follows that the freedom of God comes to earth not through crowns—that is to say, through the struggle for power—but through love and solidarity with the powerless.[36]

The Christian can never be content as long as his brother is enslaved. He must suffer with him, knowing that freedom for Christ is always freedom for the oppressed. Christian freedom has its beginning "in the midst of all the misery of this world," and we "can only demonstrate this freedom by using our own freedom for the actual liberation of man from his real misery." [37]

5. *Freedom and Blackness.* What does freedom mean when we relate it to contemporary America? Because blackness is at once the symbol of oppression

---

[36] Moltmann, *op. cit.*, p. 54.
[37] *Ibid.*

and of the certainty of liberation, freedom means an affirmation of blackness. To be free is to be black, that is, identified with the victims of humiliation in human society and a participant in the liberation of man. The free man in America is the man who does not tolerate whiteness but fights against it, knowing that it is the source of human misery. The free man is the black man living in an alien world but refusing to behave according to its expectations.

Being free in America means accepting blackness as the only possible way of existing in the world. It means defining one's identity by the marks of oppression. It means rejecting white proposals for peace and reconciliation, saying, "All we know is, we must have justice, not next week but this minute."

Nat Turner, Gabriel Prosser, and Denmark Vesey are examples of free men. They realized that freedom and death were inseparable. The mythic value of their existence for the black community is incalculable, because they represent the personification of the possibility of being in the midst of nonbeing—the ability to be black in the presence of whiteness. Through them we know that freedom is what happens to black people when they decide that whitey has gone too far, and that it is incumbent upon them as the victims of humiliation to do something about the encroachment of the white thing. Freedom is the black movement of a people getting ready to liberate themselves, knowing that they cannot be unless the oppressors cease to be.

When blackness is equated with freedom as a symbol both of oppression and of the possibility of man, white people feel left out of things. "What about the oppression of whites?" they ask. "Is it not true that the enslaver also enslaves himself which makes him a member of the community of the oppressed?" There is a danger inherent in these questions. If white intellectuals, religionists, and assorted liberals can convince themselves that the white condition is analogous to the black condition, then there is no reason to respond to the demands of the black community. "After all, we are all oppressed," they say, rationalizing with a single stroke the whole white way of life. By equating their own condition with the condition of the black ghetto they are able to sleep at night, assuring themselves that we are all in the same boat.

Black Theology rejects this technique as the work of the white Christ whose basic purpose is to soothe the guilt feelings of white overlords. Inherent in the recognition of the oppressed condition is the rebellion against it with all one's might. To know oppression is to refuse to put up with it. This is why black oppression and liberation are a manifestation of the revelation of God. To be oppressed means that one is enslaved against his will by alien forces; and liberation means that one is willing to pay the cost of freedom— including death. Now we put the question to our white suburbanites: "What power is keeping you out there? Is it not true that the so-called oppression of which you speak is freely accepted because you are unwilling to pay the price for real freedom?" The basic difference between black oppression and so-called white oppression is the fact that the latter is voluntarily chosen and the former is forced upon the black community. White people can leave their ghetto whenever they please, while black people are confined against their will. Black suffering is not by choice but is a result of the evil of white people, who happen to believe that they have the first, last, and only word on how the world ought to be run.

This is not to deny that whites are enslaved. What we deny is their ability to know and analyze their slavery. The depravity of the oppressors is their enslavement to their own "freedom." Since they are free to do what they will to the oppressed, the only check being their pious feelings about the world, it is not possible for them to see the oppressed or themselves as human beings. The oppressed become objects to be used to make the world more amenable to the whims of the masters. Thus the oppressors are enslaved and dehumanized by their own will to power. They storm the citadel of the gods, claiming sole authority to declare what is real and right, and to shape the world accordingly. If they are to be liberated from such megalomania, it must be done by the oppressed. When the oppressed affirm their freedom by refusing to behave according to the masters' rules, they not only liberate themselves from oppression, but they also liberate the oppressors from an enslavement to their illusions. Therefore, the basic error of white comments about their own oppression is the assumption that they *know* the nature of their enslavement. This cannot be so, because if they really knew, they would liberate themselves by joining the revolution of the black community. They would destroy themselves and be born again as beautiful black people.

Man as a Fallen Creature

The fallenness of man is expressed in the Bible as sin. Sin is a theological concept that describes the separation of man from the source of his being. Instead of affirming his identity in the source of being, man rejects it and attempts to be what he is not. Sin is thus a definition of being in relation to nonbeing; it is a condition of estrangement from the source of meaning and purpose in the universe.

1. Sin as a Community Concept. In order to understand clearly the function of sin in the biblical tradition, it is necessary to point out that it is meaningful only in the context of the Israelite community. Sin is not an abstract idea that defines ethical behavior for all men. Rather it is a religious concept that defines the condition of man as he is separated from the essence of the community. To be in sin has nothing to do with the disobedience of laws that are alien to the community's existence. Quite the contrary, the failure to destroy those powers that seek to enforce alien laws on the community is to be in a state of sin. It is incumbent on all members of the community to define their existence according to the community's essence and to defend the community against that which seeks to destroy it. To be in sin, then, is to deny the values that make the community what it is. It is living according to one's private interests and not according to the goals of the community. It is believing that one can live independently of that source that is responsible for the community's existence.

For Israel sin meant an alienation from the covenant of Yahweh as grounded in his liberating activity at the Exodus. If the meaning of Israel's existence is defined by the Exodus and the covenant, then all other ways of living in the world must be termed a violation of her existence as the people of Yahweh. Sin in the community of Israel is nothing but a refusal to acknowledge the significance of the Exodus and the covenant as God's liberating activity. It means grounding one's being on some loyalty other than Yahweh. It is counting his activity as secondary by refusing to define the community in terms of divine liberation.

It is man's existence in community that defines the meaning of sin. To be in sin means to deny the community. Nor does this definition of sin ignore the biblical claim that the Fall describes the condition of *all* men. Indeed that is the very point: Genesis 3 is *Israel's* analysis of universal sin and thus is comprehensible only from her perspective. It is not likely that other communities, who have defined their being from other sources, will take too seriously Israel's condemnation of them as sinners. Genesis 3 is meaningful to those who participate in Israel's community and to no one else. It is important to point out that Genesis 3 was probably written during the reign of Solomon, more than three centuries after the Exodus. Casting his eye back across that time span, the writer sees Israel's history as the history of alienation from the source of her being, the Exodus and Sinai events. This historical and existential alienation is then projected onto a cosmic and universal screen in Genesis 3. Because Israel has not defined her existence exclusively according to divine liberation, she is separated from God and is in a condition of fallenness.

At the Exodus, Yahweh reveals himself as the God of oppressed Israel through his freeing them from the Egyptians. The covenant at Sinai is the agreement between Yahweh and this people that he would not cease his liberating activity if Israel would now define her existence as community on the basis of his activity of liberation. Sin then is the failure of Israel to recognize the liberating work of God. It is believing that liberation is not the definition of man's being in the world. When Israel tries to define her existence according to the pattern of other nations and thus believes that her existence is dependent on some source other than Yahweh's liberating activity, her existence is in a state of sin. To revolt against the community's reason for being is to deny the reality of the community itself. The idea of sin is applicable for other men as they are related to the community of Israel. Since Israel believes that Yahweh is Lord of all history, men who fail to define their existence accordingly are separated from God. To fail to recognize God's activity as defined by the community of Israel is to exist in sin.

The relationship between the idea of sin and community is further evident in the character of Israelite prophecy. A prophet is one who speaks for Yahweh by reminding the community of its reason for being in the world. Nathan rebukes David because he acted for self and not for the community. Elijah challenges Ahab because he fails to recognize the absolute sovereignty of Yahweh. Amos and Hosea also remind Israel of the meaning of its existence by pointing back to the Exodus and covenant. The essence of their concern is to call the community back to the source of its life. They are saying that unless we *become* what we *are* we will no longer be. Sin is living a lie, that is, trying to be what we are not. To be is to know that one's being is grounded in God's liberating activity.

The same perspective is also found in the New Testament. Because Jesus Christ, the Oppressed One, reveals to us what we are as God created us to be, the oppressed Christian community knows that as we actually *are* we are fallen creatures. We are not what we ought to be. When we look at Christ, then we know that instead of affirming our existence in him, we have denied him and taken a course completely alien to our being.

Sin then is a condition of human existence in which man denies the essence of God's liberating activity as revealed in Jesus Christ. It is a way of life in which man ceases to be man and makes choices according to his private interests, identifying the ultimate with an alien power. It is accepting slavery as a condition of human existence by denying the freedom which is grounded in God's activity. Sin is an alienation from the source of humanity in the world, resulting in human oppression and misery.

2. *Sin and the Black and White Communities*. What does sin mean for the black and white communities in contemporary America? Because sin is a concept that is meaningful only for an oppressed community as it reflects upon its liberation, it is not possible to make a universal analysis that is meaningful for both black and white people. Black Theology believes that the true nature of sin is perceived only in the moment of oppression and liberation. This means that black people, like Israel of old, know what sin is because they have experienced the source of their being and are now able to analyze their own existence in relation to the world at large. They know what nonbeing (sin) is because they have experienced being (Black Power). We are

now in a position to say what the world ought to be in relation to what it is.

Since sin is inseparable from revelation, and since revelation is an event that takes place in the moment of liberation from oppression, there can be no knowledge of the sinful condition except in the movement of an oppressed community claiming its freedom. This means that white people, despite their self-proclaimed religiousness, are rendered incapable of making valid judgments on the character of sin. That is why American theology discusses sin in the abstract, debating it in relation to universal man. In white theology, sin is a theoretical idea and not a concrete reality. No white theologian has been able to relate sin to the black and white encounter in America. Generally, white fundamentalists have identified it with moral purity. More sophisticated liberal and neo-orthodox thinkers have spoken in hushed solemnity about man's broken relation with God—but that is all they say. We are still waiting for an interpretation of sin in relation to the world at large. Invariably, white theologians analyze sin as if blacks and whites represent one community. On the one hand, Billy Graham and his cohorts are saying that the trouble with the world is that man needs God; he needs to turn from his wicked ways. The wicked ways, of course, refer to man's failure to live according to the rules of the white society. On the other hand, other whites are saying that man's problem stems from his broken relation with God—a far more serious analysis than Graham's simplistic one. But we are still waiting for the meaning of this, as black people get ready for their revolution. We wait in vain because the oppressors do not wish to know what is wrong with the world. Only the oppressed know what is wrong, because they are both the victims of evil and the recipients of God's liberating activity.

What then does sin mean for white people from the black perspective? The sin of white people is the definition of their existence in terms of whiteness. It is accepting the condition that is responsible for the Indian reservations, black concentration camps, and the rape of Vietnam. It is believing in the American way of life as defined by its history. Most white people, some despite involvement in protests, do believe in "freedom in Democracy," and they fight to make the ideals of the Constitution an empirical reality for all men. It seems that they believe that, if we just work hard enough at it, this country can be what it ought to be. But it never dawns on these do-gooders that what is wrong with America is not its failure to make the Constitution a reality for all, but rather its belief that people can be white and human at the same time. This country was founded for white people and everything that has happened in it has emerged from the white perspective. The Constitution is white, the Emancipation Proclamation was white, the government is white, business is white, the unions are white.

What we need is the destruction of whiteness, which is the source of human misery in the world.

White people fail to perceive this as the nature of sin because they are *white.* It is characteristic of sin that it permeates the whole of a man's being, distorting his humanity, leaving the sinner himself incapable of reversing the condition or indeed of truly recognizing it. If something is to be done, the action must come from another source. Christianity believes that the answer to man's condition is found in the event of Jesus Christ who meets man in his wretched condition and transforms his nonbeing into being for God. If that is true, then black confrontation with white racism is Christ himself meeting white people, providing them with the possibility of reconciliation.

Sin warps a man's existence in the world. This is what happens when a people believe that they are God's chosen people because of their high privilege in the world. It is that condition that causes ministers to compromise with slavery and to make excuses for white brutality against black people. Sin is not only the condition that produces lynchings, but it also makes white theologians define the theological enterprise as a "safe" venture. Sin is white northern congregations wondering why blacks will not come to their churches, and white southern churches fearing that blacks might come. In a word, sin is whiteness—white people's desire to be God in human relations.

What does sin mean for black people? Again, we

must be reminded that sin is a community concept, and this means that only black people can talk about their sin. The oppressors are not only rendered incapable of knowing their own condition, they cannot speak about or for the oppressed. This means that white people are not permitted to speak about what blacks have done to contribute to their condition. They cannot call blacks Uncle Toms; only members of the community can do that. To do so is not merely insensitivity, it is blasphemy! Whites cannot know us because they do not even know themselves. If we could just get "concerned" white people to recognize this fact, then we black people could get about the business of cleaning up this society by destroying the filthy manifestations of whiteness in it. To whites who want to know what they can do (a favorite question of oppressors), Black Theology says: "Keep your damn mouth closed, and let us black people get our thing together." Of course, oppressors are not used to that, and reticence is not one of their attributes. We can see that by the appearance of so many books about us by white scholars, even in religion. And the religionists seem to have an unusual dose of whiteness because they have God on their side.

If black people want to see the depth of whiteness and what it does to the distortion of truth, all they have to do is to read the two recent books on Black Power by two white fellas—Joseph Hough's *Black*

Power and White Protestants[38] and C. Freemann
Sleeper's *Black Power and Christian Responsibility*.[39]
The problem with both books is the white audacity to
speak at all, especially about Black Power. Who do
they think they are, pontificating about their brutality
against us as if they have a relevant word about black
humanity? They should know that the long history of
white silence on black liberation renders their ideas
irrelevant for both black and white people. Perhaps
their "nice" books might have been a contribution
during the eighteenth or nineteenth century, but not
today. Too much time has passed and too many
blacks have died because of the likes of this kind of
rhetoric.

But, aside from the error in sensitivity, they
missed the point altogether. Reading Sleeper and
Hough, one wonders where they have been all this
time? Where were they when Evers was assassinated,
the four children killed in the Alabama church, or
when Watts, Newark and Detroit went up in flames?
If they were *really* here, *i.e.* in touch with the reality
of the emerging Black Revolution, why do they
still speak about possibilities for "race relations"? They
should know that such talk ended some time ago.
Both men seem to assume that, if we can, as it were,
keep working on this problem, then perhaps we will

[38] New York: Oxford University Press, 1968.
[39] Nashville: Abingdon Press, 1969.

reach a solution one day. There is no attempt on their part to challenge the very essence of whiteness as an antithesis of the gospel of Christ. They still talk about "integration" as if we blacks want to assimilate with them. At any rate, they do represent the so-called advanced ways of looking at us.

If we are to understand sin and what it means to black people, it is necessary to be black and also a participant in the black liberation struggle. Because sin represents the condition of estrangement from the source of one's being, for black people this means a desire to be white and not black. It is the refusal to be what we are. Sin then for black people is the loss of identity. It is saying Yes to the white absurdity—accepting the world as it is by letting white people define black existence. To be in sin is to be contented with white solutions for the "black problem" and not rebelling against every infringement of white being on black being.

We black people know what that means because too long we have let white people determine the shape of the future and what the limits are. We have reinforced white values by letting whites define what is good and beautiful. But now we are being born anew; our community is being redeemed. This is so because we are perceiving the true nature of black existence. Black Theology's analysis of this change focuses on Jesus as the Black Christ. To this we now turn in the next chapter.

VI

Christ in Black Theology

Christian theology begins and ends with Jesus Christ. He is the point of departure for everything to be said about God, man, and the world. That is why Christology is the starting point of Karl Barth's *Dogmatics* and why Wolfhart Pannenberg says that "theology can clarify its Christian self-understanding only by a thematic and comprehensive involvement with Christological problems." [1] To speak of the Christian gospel is to speak of Christ who is the content of its message and without whom Christianity ceases to be. Therefore the answer to the question "What is the essence of Christianity?" can be given in the two words: Jesus Christ.

[1] Wolfhart Pannenberg, *Jesus—God and Man*, trans. by L. L. Wilkins and Duane A Priebe (Philadelphia: The Westminster Press, 1968), p. 11.

Because Jesus Christ is the focal point for everything that is said about the Christian gospel, it is necessary to investigate the meaning of his person and work in light of the black perspective. It is one thing to assert that he is the essence of the Christian gospel, and quite another to specify the meaning of his existence in relation to the slave ships that appeared on the American shores. Unless his existence is analyzed in light of the oppressed of the land, we are still left wondering what his presence means for the auction block, the Underground Railroad, and contemporary manifestations of Black Power. To be sure, white theology has informed us that Jesus Christ is the content of the gospel, but it has failed miserably in relating that gospel to Nat Turner, Denmark Vesey, and Gabriel Prosser. It is therefore the task of Black Theology to make theology relevant to the black reality, asking, "What does Christ mean for the oppressed blacks of the land?"

The task of explicating the existence of Christ for black people is not easy since we live in a white society that uses Christianity as an instrument of oppression. The white conservatives and liberals alike present images of a white Christ that are completely alien to the liberation of the black community. Their Christ is a mild, easy-going white American who can afford to mouth the luxuries of "love," "mercy," "long-suffering," and other white irrelevancies, because he has a multi-billion-dollar military force to protect him from the encroachments of the ghetto and the "communist conspiracy." But black existence is existence in a hostile world without the protection of the law. If Christ is to have any meaning for us, he must leave the security of the suburbs by joining black people in their condition. What need have we for a white Christ when we are not white but black? If Christ is white and not black, he is an oppressor, and we must kill him. The appearance of Black Theology means that the black community is now ready to do something about the white Christ, so that he cannot get in the way of our revolution.

The Historical Jesus and Black Theology

The investigation of the question "Who is Jesus Christ" involves the question about the historical Jesus. Since the appearance of Albert Schweitzer's *The Quest of the Historical Jesus* and the rise of the Form History School, knowledge about the historical Jesus cannot be taken for granted. During the nineteenth century, theologians assumed that the real Jesus was accessible to historical investigation, and they attempted to go behind the early church's preaching (kerygma) in order to find the authentic Jesus of Nazareth. But Schweitzer demonstrated conclusively that the liberal search for the historical Jesus was a failure and only represented the creations of men's minds. The nineteenth century "Lives" of Jesus told us more about the investigators than about Jesus himself.

Rudolf Bultmann and the form critics went even

further by suggesting that the Gospels (the only source for knowledge about Jesus) are not historical at all. The setting of the narratives is artificial, and the contents of them were created entirely by the early Christian community in order to meet its own practical needs. It is therefore foolish to imagine that it is possible to find a historical kernel within them. That is why Bultmann says that "we can know almost nothing concerning the life and personality of Jesus, since the early Christian sources show no interest in either, are moreover fragmentary and often legendary." [2]

Recently, Bultmann's radical historical skepticism has been questioned by some of his followers. The new quest for the historical Jesus began in 1953 with Ernst Käsemann's lecture, "The Problem of the Historical Jesus." According to Käsemann,

> Only if Jesus' proclamation decisively coincides with the proclamation about Jesus is it understandable, reasonable, and necessary that the Christian kerygma in the New Testament conceals the message of Jesus; only then is the resurrected Jesus the historical Jesus. From this perspective we are required, precisely as historians, to inquire behind Easter. . . . By this means we shall learn whether he stands behind the word of his church or not, whether the Christian kerygma is a myth that can be detached from his word and from himself or whether it binds us historically and insolubly to him.[3]

[2] Bultmann, *Jesus and the Word*, trans. by L. P. Smith and E. H. Lantero (New York: Charles Scribner's Sons, 1958), p. 8.
[3] Quoted in Pannenberg, *op. cit.*, p. 56.

Günther Bornkamm, Ernst Fuchs, and Hans Conzelmann joined Käsemann in his concern.[4] While all agreed that a life of Jesus is impossible, they do not agree that history is irrelevant to the Christian gospel as implied in Bultmann's analysis of New Testament mythology.[5] Bornkamm puts it this way:

> Certainly faith cannot and should not be dependent on the change and uncertainty of historical research. . . . But no one should despise the help of historical research to illumine the truth with which each of us should be concerned.[6]

Like the theologians of the new quest, Black Theology also takes seriously the historical Jesus. We want to know who Jesus *was* because we believe that that is the only way to assess who he *is*. If we have no historical information about the character and behavior of that particular Galilean in the first century, then it is impossible to determine the mode of his existence now. Without some continuity between the historical Jesus and the kerygmatic Christ, the Christian gospel becomes nothing but the subjective reflections of the early Christian community. And if that is what Christianity is all about, we not only separate it from history,

[4] For an analysis of the new quest, see James Robinson, *The New Quest of the Historical Jesus* (London: SCM Press, Ltd., 1959).

[5] See Bultmann, "New Testament and Mythology."

[6] Günther Bornkamm, *Jesus of Nazareth*, trans. by Irene and Fraser McLuskey with James Robinson (New York: Harper and Row, 1960), p. 9.

but we also allow every community the possibility of interpreting the kerygma according to its own existential situation. While the situation is important, it is not the gospel. The gospel speaks *to* the situation. Christianity believes, as Paul Tillich has suggested, that it has the answer to the existential character of the human condition. It is the function of theology to analyze the changeless gospel in such a way that it can be related to changing situations. But theology must be careful not to confuse the two. If the situation becomes paramount (*i.e.*, identified with the gospel), as it appears in Bultmann's view of the kerygmatic Christ, then there are no checks to the community's existential fancies. Black Theology also sees this as the chief error of white American religious thought, which allows the white condition to determine the meaning of Christ. The historical Jesus must be taken seriously if we intend to avoid making Christ into our own images.

Taking seriously the New Testament Jesus, Black Theology believes that the historical kernel is the manifestation of Jesus as the Oppressed One whose earthly existence was bound up with the oppressed of the land. This is not to deny that other emphases are present. Rather it is to say that whatever is said about Jesus' conduct (Fuchs), about the manifestation of the expectant eschatological future in the deeds and words of Jesus (Bornkamm), or about his resurrection as the "ultimate confirmation of Jesus' claim to authority" (Pannenberg), it must serve to illuminate Jesus' sole reason for existence: to bind the wounds of the afflicted and to liberate those who are in prison. To understand the historical Jesus without seeing his identification with the poor as decisive is to misunderstand him and thus distort his historical person. And a proper theological analysis of Jesus' historical identification with the helpless is indispensable for our interpretation of the gospel today. Unless the contemporary oppressed know that the kerygmatic Christ is the real Christ (as Martin Kähler would put it) to the extent that he was completely identified with the oppressed of his earthly ministry, they cannot know that their liberation is a continuation of his work.

The Character of the New Testament Jesus

What evidence is there that Jesus' identification with the oppressed is the distinctive historical kernel in the gospels? How do we know that Black Theology is not forcing an alien contemporary black situation on the biblical sources? These questions are important, and cannot be waved aside by black theologians. Unless we can articulate clearly an image of Christ that is consistent with the essence of the biblical message and at the same time relate it to the struggle for black liberation, Black Theology loses its reason for being. It is thus incumbent upon us to demonstrate the relationship between the historical Jesus and the oppressed, showing that the equation of the contemporary Christ with Black Power arises out of a serious encounter with the biblical revelation. Black Theology must show that the Reverend Albert Cleage's description of Jesus as the Black Messiah [7] is not the product of minds "distorted" by their own oppressed condition, but is rather the only meaningful Christological statement in our time. Any other statement about Christ is at best irrelevant and at worst blasphemous.

1. Birth. The appearance of Jesus as the Oppressed One whose existence is identified exclusively with the oppressed of the land is symbolically characterized in his birth. He was born in a stable and cradled in a manger (the equivalent of a beer case in a ghetto alley), "because there was no room for them in the inn" (Luke 2:7). Although most biblical scholars rightly question the historical validity of the birth narratives in Matthew and Luke, the mythic value of these stories is important theologically. They undoubtedly reflect the early Christian community's *historical* knowledge of Jesus as a man who defined the meaning of his existence as being one with the poor and outcasts. The visit of the shepherds, the journey of the wise men, Herod's killing of the babies, the eco-

[7] See his book published by Sheed and Ward, 1968. I should point out that my intention is not to suggest that my view of Christ is identical with Reverend Cleage's. Our perspectives do differ at points, but more importantly, we share in common the belief that *Christ is black.* It is also appropriate to express my indebtedness to his excellent work in this area.

nomic, social, and political unimportance of Mary and Joseph—all of these features reflect the early church's image of the man Jesus. For them Jesus is certainly a unique person, but the uniqueness of his appearance reveals the Holy One's concern for the lonely and downtrodden. They are not simply Matthew and Luke's explanation of the origin of Jesus' messiahship, but also a portrayal of the significance of his messiahship. His messiahship means that he is one of the humiliated and the abused, even in his birth. His eating with tax collectors and sinners, therefore, was not an accident and neither was it a later invention of the early church; rather it is an expression of the being of God himself and thus a part of Jesus' purpose for being born.

2. *Baptism and Temptation.* The baptism (affirmed by most scholars as historical) also reveals Jesus' identification with the oppressed. According to the Synoptic Gospels, John's baptism was for repentant sinners, an act which he believed provided an escape from God's messianic judgment. For Jesus to submit to John's baptism not only connects his ministry with John's but, more importantly, separates him from John. By being baptized, Jesus defines his existence as one with sinners and thus conveys the meaning of the coming kingdom. The kingdom is for the poor and not the rich; and it comes as an expression of God's love and not judgment. In baptism Jesus embraces the condition of sinners, affirming their existence as his own. He is one of

them! After the baptism, the saying "Thou art my beloved Son; with thee I am well pleased" (Mark 1:11) expresses God's approval of that very definition of Jesus' person and work.

The temptation is a continuation of the theme already expressed in the baptism. As with the birth narratives, it is difficult to recover the event as it happened, but it would be difficult to deny that the narrative is intimately related to Jesus' self-portrayal of the character of his existence. The Tempter's concern is to divert Jesus from the reality of his mission with the poor. Jesus' refusal to turn the stone into bread, or to worship the Tempter, or to throw himself from the pinnacle of the temple (Luke 4:3–12) may be interpreted as his refusal to identify himself with any of the available modes of oppressive or self-glorifying power. His being in the world is as one of the humiliated, suffering poor.

3. *Ministry.* The Galilean ministry is an actual working out of the decision already expressed in his birth and reaffirmed at the baptism and temptation. Mark describes the implication of this decision: "Now after John was arrested, Jesus came into Galilee, preaching the gospel of God, and saying, 'The time is fulfilled, and the kingdom of God is at hand; repent and believe in the gospel'" (Mark 1:14–15). New Testament scholars have spent many hours debating the meaning of this passage, which sometimes gives the average person the impression that there is a hid-

den meaning available only to seminary graduates. But the meaning is clear enough for those who are prepared for a radical decision about their movement in the world. Jesus' proclamation of the kingdom is an announcement of God's decision about oppressed man. "The time is fulfilled, and the kingdom of God is at hand," that is, slavery is about to end, since the reign of God displaces all false authorities. To "repent and believe in the gospel" is to recognize the importance of the hour at hand and to accept the reality of the new age by participating in it as it is revealed in the words and work of Jesus. The kingdom is Jesus, whose relation to God and man is defined by his words and work.

From this it is clear that Jesus' restriction of the kingdom to the poor has far-reaching implications for our understanding of the gospel message. It is interesting, if not surprising, to watch white New Testament scholars explain away the real theological significance of Jesus' teachings on the kingdom and the poor. Nearly always they are at pains to emphasize that Jesus did not necessarily mean the economically poor but rather, as Matthew says, "the poor in spirit." Then they proceed to point out the exceptions: Joseph of Arimathea was a rich man (Matthew 27:57) and he was "a good and righteous man" (Luke 23:50). There are also instances of Jesus' association with wealthy men; and Zacchaeus did not promise to give up *all* of his goods but only *half*. As one biblical scholar put it:

It was not so much the possession of riches as one's attitude towards them and the use one makes of them which
was the special object of Jesus' teachings and this is true
of the biblical teachings as a whole. Jesus does not condemn private property, nor is he a social reformer in any
primary sense; he is concerned with men's motives and
hearts.[8]

With all due respect to erudite New Testament
scholars and the excellent work that has been done in
this field, I cannot help but conclude that they are
"straining out a gnat and swallowing a camel"! It is
this kind of false interpretation that leads to the oppression of the poor. As long as the oppressor can be
sure that the gospel does not threaten his social, economic and political security, he can enslave men in the
name of Christ. The history of "Christianity," at least
from the time of Constantine, is a history of human enslavement; and even today, white "Christians" see little
contradiction between wealth and the Christian gospel.
It seems clear that the overwhelming weight of biblical
teaching, especially the prophetic tradition in which
Jesus stood unambiguously, is upon God's unqualified
identification with the poor precisely because they are
poor. The kingdom of God is for the helpless, because
they have no security in this world. We see this emphasis in the repeated condemnation of the rich, nota-

[8] Alan Richardson, "Poor," in Alan Richardson, ed., *Theological
Word Book of the Bible* (New York: The Macmillan Co., 1960), pp.
168-169.

bly in the Sermon on the Mount, and in Jesus' exclu-
sive identification of his ministry with sinners. The
kingdom demands the surrender of one's whole life.
How is it possible to be rich, seeing others in a state of
economic deprivation, and at the same time insist that
one has complete trust in God? Again, how can it be
said that Jesus was not primarily a social reformer but
"concerned with men's motives and hearts," when the
kingdom itself strikes across all boundaries—social, economic and political?

Jesus' teaching about the kingdom is the most radical, revolutionary aspect of his message. It involves the
totality of a man's existence in the world and what that
means in an oppressive society. To repent is to affirm
the reality of the kingdom by refusing to live on the
basis of any definition except according to the kingdom. Nothing else matters! The kingdom then is the
rule of God breaking in like a ray of light, usurping the
powers that be that hold humans as captives. That is
why exorcisms are so prominent in Jesus' ministry. They
are a visible manifestation of the presence of the kingdom. "If it is by the finger of God that I cast out de-
mons, then the kingdom of God has come upon you"
(Luke 11:20). Jesus is the Oppressed One whose work
is that of liberating humanity from inhumanity.
Through him the oppressed are set free to be what
they are. This and this alone is the meaning of his *finality* which has been camouflaged in debates about his
humanity and divinity.

4. Death and Resurrection. The death and resurrection of Jesus are the consummation of his earthly ministry with the poor. The Christian church rightly focuses on these events as decisive for an adequate theological interpretation of Jesus' historical ministry. Rudolf Bultmann pointed this out convincingly. While post-Bultmannians generally do not agree with Bultmann's extreme skepticism regarding history, they do agree on his assessment of the importance of the death-resurrection event in shaping the church's view of the earthly ministry of Jesus. The Jesus of history is not simply a figure of the past but the Christ of today as interpreted by the theological significance of the death-resurrection event. Black Theology certainly agrees with this emphasis on the cross and resurrection. The Gospels are not biographies of Jesus; they are *gospel,* that is, good news about what God has done in the life, death, and resurrection of Jesus. This must be the focus of Christological thinking.

The theological significance of the cross and resurrection is what makes the life of Jesus more than just the life of a good man who happened to like the poor. *The finality of Jesus lies in the totality of his existence in complete freedom as the Oppressed One, who reveals through his death and resurrection that God himself is present in all dimensions of human liberation.* His death is the revelation of the freedom of God, taking upon himself the totality of human oppression; his resurrection is the disclosure that God is not defeated by oppression but transforms it into the possibility of freedom. For men and women who live in an oppressive society this means that they do not have to behave as if *death* is the ultimate. God in Christ has set us free from death, and we can now live without worrying about social ostracism, economic insecurity or political death. "In Christ the immortal God has tasted death and in so doing . . . destroyed death." [9] (Compare Hebrews 2:14 ff.)

Christian freedom is the recognition that Christ has conquered death. Man no longer has to be afraid of dying. To live as if death has the last word is to be enslaved and thus controlled by the forces of destruction. The free man is the oppressed man who says No to oppressors, in spite of the threat of death, because God has said Yes to him, thereby placing him in a state of freedom. He can now deny any values that separate him from the reality of his new being. Moltmann is correct when he speaks of the resurrection as the "symbol of protest."

> To believe in the resurrection transforms faith from a deliverance from the world into an initiative that changes the world and makes those who believe into wordly, personal, social and political witnesses to God's righteousness and freedom in the midst of a repressive society and an unredeemed world. In this, faith comes to historical self-consciousness and to the recognition of its eschatological task within history.[10]

[9] Richardson, "Death," in *ibid.*, p. 60.
[10] "Toward a Political Hermeneutic of the Gospel," *Union Theological Seminary Quarterly Review*, Vol. XXIII, No. 4 (Summer, 1968), pp. 211, 312.

The Black Christ

What is the significance of the historical and resurrected Christ for our times? The answer to this question must focus on both the meaning of the historical Jesus and the contemporary significance of the resurrection. It is impossible to gloss over either one of these emphases and still retain the gospel message.

Focusing on the historical Jesus means that Black Theology recognizes *history* as the indispensable foundation of Christology. We are not free to make Christ what we wish him to be at certain moments of existence. He *is* who he *was,* and we know who he was through a critical, historical evaluation of the New Testament Jesus. Black Theology takes seriously Pannenberg's comment that "faith primarily has to do with what Jesus was." [11]

To focus on the contemporary significance of the resurrection means that we do not take Pannenberg's comment on the historical Jesus as seriously as he does. No matter how seriously we take the carpenter from Nazareth, there is still the existential necessity to relate his person to black persons, asking, "What is his relevance to the black community today?" In this sense, unlike Pannenberg, we say that the soteriological value of Christ's person must finally determine our Christol-

[11] Pannenberg, *op. cit.,* p. 28.

ogy. It is the oppressed community in the situation of liberation that determines the meaning and scope of Jesus Christ. We know who Jesus *was* and *is* when we encounter the brutality of oppression in his community as it seeks to be what it is, in accordance with his resurrection. The Christological significance of Jesus Christ is not an abstract question to be solved by intellectual debates among seminary professors. The meaning of Christ is an existential question. We know who he is when our own lives are placed in a situation of oppression, and we thus have to make a decision for or against our condition. To say No to oppression and Yes to liberation is to encounter the existential significance of the Resurrected One. He is the Liberator *par excellence* whose very presence makes persons sell all that they have and follow him.

Now what does this mean for black people in America today? How are they to interpret the Christological significance of the Resurrected One in such a way that his Person will be existentially relevant to their oppressed condition? Since the black community is an oppressed community because, and only because, of its blackness, the Christological importance of Jesus Christ must be found in his blackness. If he is not black as we are, then the resurrection has little significance for our times. Indeed, if he cannot be what we are, we cannot be who he is. Our being with him is dependent on his being with us in the oppressed black condition, revealing to us what is necessary for our liberation.

The definition of Christ as black is crucial for Christology if we truly believe in his continued presence today. Taking our clue from the historical Jesus who is pictured in the New Testament as the Oppressed One, what else, except blackness, could adequately tell us the meaning of his presence today? Any statement about Christ today that fails to consider blackness as the *decisive* factor about his Person is a denial of the New Testament message. The life, death and resurrection of Jesus reveal that he is the man for others, disclosing to them what is necessary for their liberation from oppression. If this is true, then Christ must be black with black people so they can know that their liberation is his liberation.

The Black Christ is also an important theological symbol for an analysis of Christ's presence today because we must make decisions about where he is at work in the world. Is his presence synonymous with the work of the oppressed or the oppressors, blacks or whites? Is he to be found among the wretched or among the rich? Of course our clever white theologians would say that it is not either/or. Rather he is to be found somewhere in between, a little black and a little white. Such an analysis is not only irrelevant for our times but also irrelevant for the time of the historical Jesus. Jesus was not for and against the poor, for and against the rich. He was for the poor and against the rich, for the weak and against the strong. Who can read the New Testament and fail to see that Jesus took sides and accepted freely the problem of being misunderstood? If the historical Jesus is any clue for an analysis of the contemporary Christ, then he must be where men are enslaved. To speak of him is to speak of the liberation of the oppressed. In a society that defines blackness as evil and whiteness as good, the theological significance of Jesus is found in the possibility of human liberation through blackness. Jesus is the Black Christ!

Concretely, to speak of the presence of Christ today means focusing on the forces of liberation in the black community. Value perspectives must be reshaped in the light of what aids the self-determination of black people. The definition of Christ as black means that he is the complete opposite of the values of white culture. He is the center of a black Copernican revolution. Black Theology seeks to do in American Theology what Copernicus did to man's thinking about the physical universe. Since this country has achieved its sense of moral and religious idealism by oppressing blacks, the Black Christ leads the warfare against the white assault on blackness by striking at white values and white religion. The black Copernican revolution means extolling as good what whites have ignored or regarded as evil.

The blackness of Christ clarifies the definition of him as the *Incarnate* One. In him God becomes oppressed man and thus reveals that the achievement of full humanity is consistent with his being. Man was not created to be a slave, and the appearance of God in Christ provides man with the possibility of freedom. By becoming a black man, God discloses that blackness is not what the world says it is. Blackness is a manifestation of the being of God in that it reveals that neither divinity nor humanity reside in white definitions but in the liberation of man from captivity. The Black Christ is he who threatens the structure of evil as seen in white society, rebelling against it, thereby becoming the embodiment of what the black community knows that it must become. Because he has become black as we are, we now know what black empowerment is. It is black people determining the way they are going to behave in the world. It is refusing to allow white society to place strictures on black existence as if their having guns mean that blacks are suppose to cool it. Black empowerment is the black community in defiance, knowing that he who has become one of them is far more important than threats from white officials. The Black Christ is he who nourishes the rebellious impulse in black people, so that at the appointed time the black community can respond collectively to the white community as a corporate "bad nigger," lashing out at the enemy of man.

It is to be expected that some whites will resent the Christological formulation of the Black Christ, either by ignoring it or by viewing it as too narrow to include the universal note of the gospel. It will be difficult for white people to deny the whiteness of their existence and affirm the oppressed Black Christ. But the concept of black, which includes both what the world means by oppression and what the gospel means by liberation, is the only concept that has any real significance today. If Christ is not black, then who is he? We could say that he is the Son of God, Son of Man, Messiah, Lord, Son of David and a host of other titles. The difficulty with these titles is not that they fail to describe the Person of Christ, but they are first-century titles. To cling to them without asking, "What appropriate symbol do these titles refer to today?" is to miss the significance of them altogether. What is striking about the New Testament names of Jesus is the dimension of liberation embedded in them. For example, Christ as Lord, a post-resurrection title, emphasizes his complete authority over all creation. Everyone is subject to him. The Lord is the "ruler," "commander," he who has all authority. If "Jesus is Lord," as one of the earliest baptismal creeds of the Church puts it, then what does this say about black and white relations in America? The meaning is perhaps too obvious for comment. It means simply that white people do not have authority over black people. Our loyalty belongs only to him who has become like us in everything, especially blackness. To take seriously the Lordship of Christ or his Sonship or Messiahship is to see him as the sole criterion for authentic existence. If he is the Suffering Servant of God, he is an oppressed man who has taken on that very form of human existence that is responsible for human misery. What we need to ask is this: "What is the form of humanity that accounts for human suffering in our society? What is it, except blackness?" If Christ is truly the Suffering Servant of God who takes upon himself the suffering of his people, thereby reestablishing the covenant of God, then he must be black. To get at the meaning of this and not get bogged down in racial emotionalism, we need only to ask, "Is it possible to talk about suffering in America without talking about the meaning of blackness? Can we really believe that Christ is the Suffering Servant *par excellence* if he is not black?" Black Theology contends that blackness is the one symbol that cannot be overlooked if we are going to take seriously the Christological significance of Jesus Christ.

But some whites will ask, Does Black Theology believe that Christ was *really* black? It seems to me that the *literal* color of Jesus is irrelevant, as are the different shades of blackness in America. Generally speaking, black people are not oppressed on the basis of the depths of their blackness. "Light" blacks are oppressed just as much as "black" blacks. But as it happens, *he was not white* in any sense of the word, literally or theologically. Therefore, the Reverend Cleage is not too far wrong when he describes Jesus as a black Jew; and he is certainly on solid theological grounds when he describes him as the Black Messiah.

The importance of the concept of the Black Christ is

that it expresses the *concreteness* of Christ's continued presence today. If we do not translate the first-century titles into symbols that are relevant today, then we run the danger that Bultmann is so concerned about: Christ merely becomes a figure of past history. To make Christ just a figure of yesterday is to deny the real importance of the early church's preaching. He is not dead but resurrected and is alive in the world today. Like yesterday, he has taken upon himself the misery of his people, becoming to them what is needed for their liberation. To be a disciple of the Black Christ is to become black with him. Looting, burning, or the destruction of so-called white property are not *primary* concerns. Such matters can only be decided by the oppressed themselves who are seeking to develop their images of the Black Christ. What is primary is that blacks must refuse to let whites define what is appropriate for the black community. Just as white slaveholders in the nineteenth century said that questioning slavery was an invasion of their property rights, so today they use the same line of reasoning in reference to black self-determination. But Nat Turner had no scruples on this issue; and blacks today are beginning to see themselves in a new image. We believe in the manifestation of the Black Christ, and our encounter with him defines our values. This means that blacks are *free* to do what they have to in order to affirm their humanity.

The Kingdom of God and the Black Christ

The appearance of Jesus as the Black Christ also means that the Black Revolution is God's kingdom becoming a reality in America. According to the New Testament, the kingdom is a historical event. It is what happens to a person when his being is confronted with the reality of God's historical liberation of the oppressed. To see the kingdom is to see a happening, and we are thus placed in a situation of decision—we say either Yes or No to the liberation struggle.

The kingdom is not an attainment of material security, nor is it mystical communion with the divine. It has to do with the *quality* of one's existence in which a person realizes that *persons* are more important than property. When black people behave as if the values of this world have no significance, that means that they perceive the irruption of God's kingdom. The kingdom of God is a *black* happening. It is black people saying No to whitey, retreating into caucuses and advancing into white confrontation. It is a beautiful thing to see black people shaking loose the chains of white approval, and it can only mean that they know that there is a way of living that does not involve the destruction of their persons. This is the kingdom of God.

For Jesus, repentance is a precondition for entrance into the kingdom. But it should be pointed out that repentance has nothing to do with morality or religious piety in the white sense. Günther Bornkamm's analysis of Jesus' call to repentance is relevant here. To repent, says Bornkamm, is "to lay hold on the salvation which is already at hand, and to give up everything for it." [12] It means recognizing the importance of the kingdom-event and casting one's lot with it. The kingdom is God's own event and inherent in its appearance is the invitation to renounce everything and join it. That is why Jesus said, "If your hand or your foot causes you to sin, cut it off and throw it from you; it is better for you to enter life maimed or lame than with two hands or two feet to be thrown into eternal fire. And if your eye causes you to sin, pluck it out and throw it from you; it is better for you to enter life with one eye than with two eyes to be thrown into the hell of fire" (Matthew 18:8–9).

According to Bornkamm,

> repentance comes by means of grace. Those who sit at the table of the rich lord are the poor, the cripples, the blind and lame, not those who are already half-cured. The tax collectors and sinners with whom Jesus sits at meat are not asked first about the state of their moral improvement. . . . The extent to which all talk of the conditions which man must fulfill before grace is accorded him is here silenced, as shown by the parables of the lost sheep and the lost coin, which tell only of the finding of what was lost, and in this very manner describe the joy in heaven "over one sinner who repents" (Luke 15:7, 10). So little is repentance a human action

[12] Bornkamm, *op. cit.*, p. 82.

preparing the way for grace that it can be placed on the
level of being found.[13]

The kingdom is what God does and repentance arises
solely as a response to his liberation.

The event of the kingdom today is the liberation
struggle in the black community. It is where people
are suffering and dying for want of human dignity. It is
thus incumbent upon all to see the event for what it is
—God's kingdom. This is what conversion means. Black
people are being converted because they see in the
events around them the coming of the Lord, and will
not be scared into closing their eyes to it. Black identity is too important; it is like the pearl of great value,
which a man buys only by selling all that he has (Matthew 13:44–46).

Of course, whites can say that they fail to see the
significance of this black phenomenon. But the loss of
sight is characteristic of the appearance of the kingdom. Not everyone recognizes the man from Nazareth
as the incarnate Lord who came to liberate men. Who
could possibly imagine that the Holy One of Israel
would condescend to the level of a carpenter? Only
those with eyes of faith could see that in that man God
himself was confronting the reality of the human condition. There is no other sign save the words and deeds
of Jesus himself. If an encounter with him does not
convince persons that God is present, then they will

[13] *Ibid.*, pp. 83–84.

never know, except in that awful moment when perfect awareness is fatally bound up with irreversible judgment. That is why Jesus compared the kingdom with a mustard seed and with yeast in bread dough. Both show a small, apparently insignificant beginning and a radical, revolutionary ending. The seed grows to a large tree, and the bread is able to feed many people. So it is with the kingdom; because of its small beginning, men do not readily perceive what is actually happening.

The black revolution is a continuation of that small kingdom. Whites do not recognize what is happening, and they are thus unable to deal with it. For most whites in power, the black community is a nuisance—something to be considered only when the natives get restless. But what white America fails to realize is the explosive nature of the kingdom. Although its beginning is small, it will have far-reaching effect not only on the black community but on the white community as well. Now is the time to make decisions about loyalties, because soon it will be too late. Shall we or shall we not join the Black Revolutionary kingdom?

To enter the kingdom is to enter the state of salvation, the condition of blessedness. Historically it appears that "salvation" is Paul's translation of Jesus' phrase "kingdom of God." But, oh, how the word "salvation" has been beaten and battered in nineteen centuries of Christian verbiage! What can salvation possibly mean for oppressed blacks in America? Is it a kind of spiritual juice, squirted into the life of the dispirited that somehow enables them to withstand the brutality of the oppressors because they know that heaven is waiting for them? Certainly, this is what rulers would like for the oppressed to believe. In most societies where political oppression is acute and religion is related to the state, salvation is interpreted always in ways that do not threaten the security of the existing government. Sometimes salvation takes the form of abstract, intellectual analysis or private mystical communion with the divine. The "hope" that is offered the oppressed is not the possibility of changing their earthly condition but a longing for the next life. With the poor counting on salvation in the next life, the oppressors can humiliate and exploit without fear of reprisal. That is why Karl Marx called religion the opiate of the people. It is an open question whether he was right in his evaluation; but he was correct in identifying the oppressors' intention. They promote religion because it can be an effective tool for enslavement.

The history of the black church is a case in point. At first, white "Christian" slaveholders in America did not allow their slaves to be baptized because Christianity supposedly enfranchised them. But because the white church was having few converts among blacks, it proceeded to assure the slaveholders that baptism had nothing to do with civil freedom. In fact, many white ministers assured the masters that Christianity would make them better slaves. With that assurance, the masters began to introduce Christianity to blacks, confident that it would make blacks more obedient. But many blacks were able to appropriate the white Christianity for their own condition by turning it into a religion of revolution. The organization of the African Methodist Episcopal Church and the African Methodist Episcopal Zion Church with other black independent religious institutions, together with their involvement in the antislavery movement, shows that black religionists did see through the fake white Christianity of the period. For the pre-Civil War black church salvation involved more than the longing for the next life. Being saved was also a present reality that placed persons in a dimension of freedom so that earthly injustice became intolerable. That was why Nat Turner, a Baptist preacher, had visions of God that involved his own election to be the Moses of his people, leading them from the house of bondage. After his insurrection black preachers were outlawed in the South.

Unfortunately, the post-Civil War black church fell into the white trick of interpreting salvation in terms similar to those of the white oppressors. Salvation became white: an objective act of Christ in which God "washes" away our sins in order to prepare us for a new life in heaven. The resurgence of the black church in civil rights and the creation of a Black Theology represent an attempt of the black community to see salvation in the light of their own earthly liberation.

The interpretation of salvation as liberation from

bondage is certainly consistent with the biblical view. "In the Old Testament salvation is expressed by a word which has the root meaning of 'to be wide' or 'spacious' 'to develop without hindrance' and thus ultimately 'to have victory in battle' (I Sam. 14:45)." [14] To be saved meant that one's enemies have been conquered, and the savior is he who has the power to gain victory.

> He who needs salvation is one who has been threatened or oppressed, and his salvation consists in deliverance from danger and tyranny or rescue from imminent peril (I Sam. 4:3, 7:8, 9:16). To save another is to communicate to him one's own prevailing strength (Job 26:2), to give him the power to maintain the necessary strength.[15]

In Israel, God himself is the Saviour par excellence. Beginning with the Exodus, his righteousness is for those who are weak and helpless. "The mighty work of God, in which his righteousness is manifested, is in saving the humble . . . the poor and the dispirited." [16] The same is true in the New Testament. Salvation is from slavery to freedom (Galatians 5:1, II Corinthians 3:17), from fear of principalities and powers to liberty (I John 4:18). This is not to deny that salvation is a future reality; but it is hope that focuses on the present.

In our language today, the oppressed are the people of the black ghettos, the Indian reservations, the Span-

---

[14] F. J. Taylor, "Save," in Richardson, op. cit., p. 219.
[15] Ibid.
[16] Ibid.

ish *barrios,* and other places where whiteness has created misery. To participate in God's salvation is to co-operate with the Black Christ as he liberates his people from bondage. Salvation then primarily has to do with earthly reality and the injustice inflicted on those who are helpless and poor. To see the salvation of God is to see this people rise up against their oppressors, demanding that justice become a reality now and not tomorrow. It is the oppressed serving warning that they "ain't gonna take no more of this bullshit, but a new day is coming and it ain't going to be like today." The new day is the presence of the Black Christ as expressed in the liberation of the black community.

VII

Church, World and Eschatology in Black Theology

Carl Michalson once said:

> The Christian Gospel is a proclamation which strikes the ear of the world with the force of a hint. Some "get it"; some do not. To those who do, it is "the power of God unto salvation." To those who do not, it can seem a scandal and offence! [1]

The Christian church is that community of persons who "got the hint," and they thus refuse to be content with human pain and suffering. To receive

[1] Carl Michalson, *Worldly Theology* (New York: Charles Scribner's Sons, 1967), p. 184.

"the power of God unto salvation" places persons in a state of Christian existence, making it impossible for them to sit still as their neighbors are herded off to prison camps. The hint of the gospel moves them to say No to rulers of the world, saying, "If our brothers have to go, it will be over our dead bodies." These are the people who believed in the gospel of liberation, resolving that the freedom of persons is more important than "law and order." Only a few decades ago, Hitler and his demigods exterminated over six million Jews in the name of "law and order." In words very similar to the language of our own politicians, he said:

The streets of our country are in turmoil. The universities are filled with students rebelling and rioting. Communists are seeking to destroy our country. Russia is threatening us with her might and the republic is in danger. Yes, danger from within and from without. *We need law and order.* Yes, without law and order our nation cannot survive. Elect us and we will restore law and order. We shall by law and order be respected among the nations of the world. Without law and order our republic shall fail.[2]

Because the church is that community that participates in Christ's liberating work in history, it can never endorse "law and order" while people are suffering. To do so is to say Yes to structures of oppression. Since it

[2] Quoted in L. I. Stell, "Changing of the Guard," *Tempo*, Vol. 2, No. 9, February 15, 1969, p. 3 (Hitler's Campaign Speech, 1932).

has received the gospel-hint and has accepted what that means for human existence, the church must be a revolutionary community, breaking laws that destroy persons. It believes (with Reinhold Niebuhr) that "comfortable classes may continue to dream of an automatic progress in society. They do not suffer enough from social injustice to recognize its peril in the life of society." [3]

In the New Testament the church (ecclesia) is that community that has received the Holy Spirit and is now ready to do what is necessary to live out the gospel. They are the people who have become heirs of the promises of God; and because they have experienced what that means for humanity, they cannot accept the world as it is. They must rebel against evil so all people may know that they do not have to behave according to societal laws.

Participating in the historical liberation of God is the defining characteristic of the church. The task of the church is threefold. First, it proclaims the reality of divine liberation. This is what the New Testament calls preaching the gospel. The gospel is the proclamation of God's liberation as revealed in the event of Jesus and the outpouring of the Holy Spirit. It is not possible to receive the good news of freedom and also keep it to ourselves; it must be told to the whole world. This is what the writer of Matthew had in mind as he records

[3] Reinhold Niebuhr, *Moral Man and Immoral Society* (New York: Charles Scribner's Sons, 1932), pp. 165-166.

Jesus as saying: "Go therefore and make disciples of all nations, baptizing them in the name of the Father and of the Son and of the Holy Spirit, teaching them to observe all that I have commanded you; and lo, I am with you always, to the close of the age." (Matthew 28:19–20).

To preach the gospel today means confronting the world with the reality of Christian freedom. It means telling black people that their slavery has come to an end, and telling whites to let go of the chains. Black people do not have to live according to white rules. If the gospel is "the power of God unto salvation," then black people have a higher loyalty to him that cuts across every sphere of human existence. Preaching the gospel is nothing but proclaiming to blacks that they do not have to submit to ghetto-existence. Our new existence has been bought and paid for; we are now redeemed, set free. Now it is incumbent upon us to behave like free persons.

Secondly, the church not only proclaims the good news of freedom, it actively shares in the liberation struggle. Though the battle against evil has been won, old rulers pretend that they are still in power. They are still trying to enforce the laws of the old order. The function of the church is to remind them that they are no longer in power. The last has become first and the first last. A Copernican revolution has taken place in human existence that transcends anything past or present. The church is that community that lives on the basis of the radical demands of the gospel by making the gospel message a social, economic and political reality. It has the courage to take the risk, knowing that, at this early stage, it lives in a society that refuses to believe the gospel message. It thus goes against the grain of societal existence because its sole aim is to share with Christ in his liberating activity.

For blacks this means that societal values are no longer important. Blacks are free to share in their brothers' liberation by making the world more receptive to blackness. We must assume that all blacks want to be free and that, if given half a chance, they will affirm the liberty that is theirs. The church means the people who make the world more amenable to black self-determination by forcing rulers to decide between blackness and death.

Thirdly, the church as a fellowship is a visible manifestation that the gospel is a reality. If the church cannot be free, if it is a distorted representation of the irruption of God's kingdom, if it lives according to the old order (as it usually has), then no one will believe its message. If someone tells me that Christ has set us free from all alien loyalties, but he himself obeys these loyalties that he claims Christ has defeated, then I must conclude that he does not really believe what he says. To believe is to live accordingly; the church must live according to its preaching. This is what Bonhoeffer had in mind when he called the church "Christ existing as a community"

The participation in divine liberation places the church squarely in the context of the world. Its existence is inseparable from worldly involvement. While Black Theology cannot say that the "church is the world" or the "world is the church" (as implied in some secular theologies), it does affirm that the church cannot be the church in isolation from the concrete realities of human suffering. The world is earthly existence, the place where people are enslaved. It is where laws are passed against the oppressed, and where the oppressed fight back even though their efforts seem futile. The world is where white and black people live, encountering each other, the latter striving for a little more room to breathe and the former doing everything possible to destroy black reality.

The world is not a metaphysical entity nor an ontological problem as some philosophers and theologians would have us believe. It is very concrete. It is punching clocks, taking orders, fighting rats and being kicked around by policemen. It is where the oppressed live. Jews encountered it in concentration camps, Indians on reservations and blacks on slave ships, in cotton fields, and in "dark" ghettos. The world is white people, the degrading rules they make for the "underprivileged," and their guilt-dispelling recourse to political and theological slogans about the welfare of the society "as a whole." In short, the world is where the brutal reality of inhumanity makes its ungodly appearance, making persons into animals.

Because the church knows that the world is where people are dehumanized, it can neither retreat from the world nor embrace it. Retreating is tantamount to a denial of its calling to share in divine liberation. It is a complete misunderstanding of the Christ-event which demands radical, worldly involvement on behalf of oppressed men. Retreating is navel-gazing, a luxury that oppressed persons cannot afford. Only oppressors can turn in upon themselves and worship their own projected image and define it as God. People who live in the world have to encounter the concreteness of suffering without suburbs as places of retreat. To be oppressed is to encounter the overwhelming presence of human evil without any place to escape. Either we submit or we rebel, knowing that our physical lives are at stake.

The church cannot seriously consider retreat as an option because its very existence is affirmed and reaffirmed only as it demonstrates to all what Christian existence is all about *in* the world. There is no place for sheltered piety. Who can "pray" when all hell has broken loose and when the gut of human existence is being trampled underfoot by evil forces? Prayer takes on new meaning. It has nothing to do with those Bible verses that rulers utter before eating their steaks, in order to remind themselves that they are religious and have not mistreated anybody. Who can thank God for food when we know that our brothers are starving as we dine like kings? Prayer is not that morning, noon and evening kneeling. This is a tradition that is characteristic of whites; they use it to reinforce the rightness of their destruction of black people. Prayer is the spirit that is evident in all oppressed communities when they know that they have a job to do. It is that communication with the divine that makes them know that they have very little to lose in the fight against evil and a lot to gain. We can only lose our physical lives but can gain what the writer of the Fourth Gospel calls eternal life and what black people call blackness. To retreat from the world is to lose one's life and become what other men say we are.

The embracing of the world is also a denial of the gospel. The history of traditional Christianity and recent secular theology show the danger of this procedure. Identifying the rise of nationalism with Christianity, capitalism with the gospel, or exploration of outer space with the advancement of the kingdom serves only to enhance the oppression of the weak. It is a denial of the Lordship of Christ. To affirm Christ as Lord means that the world stands under his judgment. There is no place or person that is not subject to his rule. And since not everyone recognizes Christ for who he is, the task of the church is to be out there in the world, not as an endorser of its oppression but as the visible representative of his Lordship. The world is where we are called to fight against evil.

The difficulty of defining the meaning of the church and its involvement in the world stems from the unchurchly behavior of institutional white churches. They have given the word "church" a bad reputation for those interested in fighting against human suffering. Because of the unchristian behavior of people who say they are Christians, "church" in America may very well refer to the respectable murderers, people who destroy human dignity while "worshipping" God and feeling no guilt about it. They equate things as they are with God's will. To think of the church in this society is to visualize buildings with crosses and signs designating Sunday morning worship. It is to think of pious white people gathering on Sunday, singing hymns and praying to God, while their preachers talk endlessly about some white cat who died on a cross. For some reason, it never enters the minds of these murderers that Christ does not approve of their behavior. Christ died not to "save" them but to destroy them, to dissolve their whiteness in the fire of judgment, for it is only through their destruction that the wholeness of humanity may be realized.

Unfortunately black churches are also guilty of prostituting the name of God's church. Having originally come into being because they knew that political involvement in societal liberation of black people was equivalent with the gospel, it is a sad fact that they all but lost their reason for being in subsequent decades. Except for rare prophetic figures like Jesse Jackson and Albert Cleage, the black denominational churches seem to be content with things as they are, getting fat off their brothers' misery. While possessing the greatest potentiality for Black Revolution, the black churches satisfy themselves with white solutions to earthly injustice. That is why people interested in justice in this world so often scorn the black church, saying that it is only a second-rate oppressor.

If the white and black churches do not represent Christ's redemptive work in the world, where then is Christ's church to be found? As always, his church is where wounds are being healed and chains are being struck off. It does not matter in the least whether the community of liberators designate their work as Christ's own work. What is important is that people are being liberated. Indeed there may be some advantages in not consciously doing anything for Christ simply because one wants to be a Christian. The truly Christian response to earthly existence is doing what one must do because it is the *human* thing to do. The brother's suffering should not be used as a stepping-stone in Christian piety. This may be what Jesus had in mind when he told the parable of the Last Judgment (Matthew 25:31 ff.). People are received and rejected according to their ministering to human need. Those who were received were surprised for they did not view their work as God's own. They were not seeking a reward. They were only doing what they considered the *human* thing to do. That is why they asked, "Lord, when did we see thee hungry and feed thee, or thirsty and give thee drink? And when did we see thee a stranger and welcome thee, or naked and clothe thee? And when did we see thee sick or in prison and visit thee?" Their actions were not meant for the King! But the King will answer, "Truly, I say to you, as you did it to one of the least of these my brethren, you did it to me." Because the work of God is not a superimposed activity but a part of one's existence as a person, the religious man is caught in a trick. He is rejected because he failed to see that being good is not a societal trait or an extra activity, but a human activity. He is excluded because he merely used the neighbor as an enhancement of his own religious piety. Had he known that black people were Jesus, he would have been prepared to relieve their suffering. But that is just the point: there is no way to know in the abstract who is Christ and who is not. It is not an intellectual question at all. Knowledge of Christ comes as one participates in the liberation of men.

What about Eschatology?

No study in systematic theology is complete which does not deal with the question of eschatology. To speak about eschatology is to move in the direction of the future, what has often been called the last things. The question about the "not yet" has always been one of man's chief questions, and its importance is symbolized in the certainty of death. All living things die; but as Reinhold Niebuhr pointed out, only man knows of his future end. It is man's knowledge of his future ceasing-to-be that makes him different from other creatures. To anticipate the certainty of nonexistence understandably places man in a state of anxiety. What can he do about death and its relation to life? If man knows that his present existence will be swallowed up by the future reality of nothingness, what can he hope for when his present being no longer is? Is there life after death?

These are tough questions, and any perspective that seeks to deal with human existence cannot sidestep them. It could be argued that the origin of religion is due to man's attempt to answer the problem of the human end. And the success of any religion in winning adherents may be traced to its ability to give a satisfactory answer to the question of death. What does the Black Theological perspective have to say about the black man's ultimate hope and its relation to his present existence in liberation? What does it have to say about death?

Black Theology rejects as invalid the oppressors' attempt to escape the question of death. The white rulers in the society seek to evade the reality of the end by devising recreational hobbies. They play golf, vacation in distant lands, live in all manner of luxury. Instead of facing up to the reality of finite existence and the anxiety that accompanies it, they pretend that their eternality is dependent on their political, social and economic dominance over the weak and helpless. With their power to control history and man's present and future relation to man, who can deny that they are not the masters of the world's destiny? It is their confidence in their own present strength that renders them incapable of looking the future squarely in the face. The oppressors do not know death because they do not know themselves—their finiteness and future end.

In contrast to the oppressors' inability to deal with death, the oppressed cannot escape their future end, for the visible presence of the rulers is a constant reminder that nonexistence may come at any moment. For black people, death is not really a future reality; it is a part of their everyday existence. They see death every time they see white people. The death of men, women and children at the hands of whites who wheel and deal in the structures of society precludes the possibility of escape from life or death. Black people then are forced to ask, what is the relation between the past, present and future in the context of the blackness of our condition?

We do not find answers to questions about life and death by reading books. Life-and-death questions are not learned questions, and the answers are not found in a theology or philosophy class. The answers to questions about the end come when we face the reality of future nonexistence in the context of existence that is characterized by oppression and liberation. *We know what the end is when we face it head-on by refusing to tolerate present injustice at the risk of death.* The proper eschatological perspective must be grounded in the historical present, thereby forcing the oppressed community to say No to unjust treatment because their present humiliation is inconsistent with their promised future.

No eschatological perspective is sufficient which does not challenge the present order. If contemplation about the future distorts the present reality of injustice and reconciles the oppressed to unjust treatment committed against them, then it is unchristian and thus has nothing whatsoever to do with him who came to liberate us. It is this that renders white talk about heaven and life after death fruitless for black people. We know all about pearly gates, golden streets and long white robes. We have sung songs about heaven until we were hoarse, but it did not change the present state or ease the pain. To be sure, we may "Walk in Jerusalem jus' like John" and "There may be a great camp meeting in the Promised Land," but we want to walk in this land —"the land of the free and the home of the brave." We want to know why cannot Harlem become Jerusalem and Chicago the Promised Land? What good are golden crowns, slippers, white robes or even eternal life, if it means that we have to turn our backs on the pain and suffering of our own children? Unless the future can become present, thereby forcing us to make changes in this world, what significance could eschatology have for black people who believe that their self-determination must become a reality *now!* White missionaries have always encouraged blacks to forget about present injustice and look forward to heavenly justice. But Black Theology says No, insisting that we either put new meaning into Christian hope by relating it to our liberation or drop it altogether.

Perhaps, a place to begin for this new eschatological significance is the theology of Rudolf Bultmann.[4] Taking his clue from the existential orientation of Martin Heidegger, Bultmann has pointed out some interesting things about theological eschatology and its relation to history. Concentrating his intellectual efforts on articulating an eschatological perspective that was consistent with the achievement of man's authentic selfhood as defined by Heidegger's philosophy, Bultmann concluded that the future of man cannot be separated from his being-in-the-present. He therefore rejected any eschatological viewpoint that centered on cosmological ingredients, or apocalyptic speculations on nonearthly reality. To accept mythology as the key to eschatology is to reject "the complete genuine historicity of man." Eschatology, said Bultmann, must focus on man as he exists in his existential situation in which the meaning of history is located in the present moment of decision.

[4] See Bultmann, *History and Eschatology* (Edinburgh: The University Press, 1957). See also his *Primitive Christianity in Its Contemporary Setting*, trans. by R. H. Fuller (London: Thames and Hudson, 1956), and his *New Testament Theology*, Vol. I, trans. by K. Grobel (New York: Charles Scribner's Sons, 1951).

Contemporary theology is indebted to Bultmann for forcing his point, namely that eschatology cannot be separated from man's present historical moment. But he did not take his point far enough. His view failed to take seriously the significance of the liberation of an oppressed community. How is eschatology related to *protest* against injustice and the need for revolutionary change? True, as Bultmann pointed out, a man's future cannot be separated from his present moment of decision. But neither can his future be separated from the future of his community, the nation. In the Old Testament, God is conceived not only as a God who acts in history *for me;* he acts in the history of a particular community. And his action can only be for me insofar as I choose to belong to his community. A man's selfhood is bound up with the community to which he belongs.

Also, Bultmann failed to point out that the future of God in biblical history cannot be separated from the *oppressed condition* of his people. Who are they that long for the coming of the Lord and for what purpose? They who wait on the Lord are they who are weak, they are the poor, the helpless and the downtrodden. The powerful have no need for God's future because they are confident that their own strength will prevail. The future of God belongs to the future of the poor, the people who are assured that God's present righteousness will not be defeated by those who seek to usurp divine authority. The poor need not worry about the evil of this world; they will see the glory of Yahweh in their own fight against injustice.

The dimension of future as protest against evil, while absent in Bultmann, may be found in the recent talk about "hope theology." [5] The "hope theologians" take their cue from Ernst Bloch, who says, "Reality does not have a definite dimension. The world is not fixed." Or again, he says, " 'Things can be otherwise.' That means: things can also *become* otherwise: in the direction of evil, which must be avoided, or in the direction of good, which would have to be promoted." [6] Eschatology is related to action and change.

However, it is Jürgen Moltmann, one of the most prominent "hope theologians," who places the Marxist emphasis on action and change in the Christian context. In his book *Theology of Hope*,[7] he says that the chief weakness of traditional thinking on eschatology is that it has been relegated to the end of time with no relation to the present. Eschatology has been interpreted as a reward to those who remain obedient. In this view, the resurrection of Christ means that salvation is now completed, finished. This accounts for the church looking at the world not as a place to die but to

[5] The phrase "hope theology" may be misleading since there is no recognizable school. For a background on these men, see Walter H. Capps, ed., "Hope," in *Cross Currents*, Vol. XVIII, no. 3 (Summer, 1968). Capps's introductory and concluding essays are excellent analyses of the mood and trends among "hope theologians."

[6] "Man as Possibility," in Capps, *op. cit.*

[7] Trans. by J. W. Leitch (New York: Charles Scribner's Sons, 1967).

live piously and prudently in preparation for the future to come. If one thinks that Christ's work is now done, then there is nothing to do but to wait for the Second Coming.

But Moltmann's concern is to show that such a view means that one has not really heard the promise of God. To hear God's promise means that the church cannot accept the present reality of things as God's intention for humanity. The future cannot be a perfection of the present. Therefore, "To know God," writes Moltmann, "is to suffer God," *i.e.*, to be called by God into the world, knowing that the present is incongruous with the expected future. "Hence it [revelation] does not give rise to powers of accommodation, but sets loose powers that are critical of being." [8] In order to guard against abstractions, Moltmann continues:

> Our hope in the promises of God . . . is not hope in God himself . . . but it hopes that his future faithfulness will bring it also the fulness of what has been promised. . . . It does not merely hope personally "in him," but has also substantial hopes of his lordship, his peace and his righteousness on earth.[9]

Moltmann's analysis is compatible with Black Theology's concern. Hope must be related to the present, and it must serve as a means of transforming an op-

[8] Moltmann, *op. cit.*, pp. 118, 119.
[9] Ibid., p. 119.

pressed community into a liberated—and liberating—community. Black Theology does not scorn Christian hope; it affirms it. It believes that, when people really believe in the resurrection of Christ and take seriously the promise revealed through him, they cannot be satisfied with the present world as it is. The past reality of the resurrection and the future of God disclosed through it makes persons restless with the imperfections of the present. It is not possible to know what the world can and ought to be and still be content with excuses for the destruction of human beings. Christians must fight against evil, for not to fight, not to do everything they can for the brother's pain is to deny the resurrection.

Christian eschatology is bound up with the resurrection of Christ. He is the eschatological hope. He is the future of God who stands in judgment upon the world and forces us to give an account of the present. In view of his victory over evil and death, why must people suffer and die? Why do we behave as if the present is a fixed reality not susceptible of radical change? As long as we look at the resurrection of Christ and the expected "end," we cannot reconcile ourselves to the things of the present that contradict his presence. It is this eschatological emphasis that Black Theology affirms.

We come back to this question again: What about life after death? On the one hand, Black Theology believes that the appearance of heaven in black churches was due primarily to white slave masters whose intention was to transfer the slaves' loyalties from earthly reality to heavenly reality. In that way, masters could do what they willed about this world, knowing that the slaves were content with life in the next world. The considerable degree to which black slaves affirmed the world view of the masters was due to their inability to change life on earth. But the rise of Black Power and Black Theology means a change in the focus of black people. We now believe that something can be done about this world, and we have resolved to die rather than deny the reality expressed in black self-determination. With this view, heaven is no longer analyzed the way it used to be. Heaven cannot mean accepting injustice of the present because we know we have a home over yonder. Home is where we have been placed *now*, and to believe in heaven is to refuse to accept hell on earth. This is one dimension of the future that cannot be sacrificed.

But there is another dimension that we must protect despite white corruption of it. Black Theology cannot reject the future reality of life after death—grounded in Christ's resurrection—simply because white people have distorted it for their own selfish purposes. That would be like the Black Art Movement, rejecting art because white artists have misused it. The task is redefinition in the light of the liberation of the black community.

If God is truly the God of and for the oppressed for

the purpose of their liberation, then the future must mean that our fight for freedom has not been for naught. Our movement in the world cannot be a meaningless thrust toward an unrealizable future, but a certainty grounded in the past and present reality of God. To grasp for the future of God is to know that those who die for freedom have not died in vain; they will see the Kingdom of God. This is precisely the meaning of our Lord's resurrection, and why we can fight against overwhelming odds. We believe in the future of God, a future that must become present.

Without a meaningful analysis of the future, all is despair. The guns, atomic power, police departments, and every conceivable weapon of destruction are in the hands of the enemy. By these standards, all seems lost. But there is another way of evaluating history; it involves the kind of perspective that enables blacks to say No in spite of the military power of their oppressors. If we really believe that death is not the last word, then we can fight, risking death for the freedom of man, knowing that man's ultimate destiny is in the hands of him who has called us into being. We do not have to worry about death if we know that it has been conquered and that as an enemy it has no efficacy. Christ's death and resurrection have set us free. Therefore it does not matter that white people have all the guns and that, militarily speaking, we have no chance of winning. *There comes a time when a people must protect their own, and for black people, the time is now.*

One last comment. The future is still the future. This means that Black Theology rejects elaborate speculations about the end. It is just this kind of speculation that led blacks to stake their whole existence on heaven—the scene of the whole company of the faithful with their long white robes. Too much of this talk is not good for the revolution. Black Theology believes that the future is God's future as are the past and present. Our past knowledge and present encounter with him are sufficient for our confidence that the future will be both like and unlike the present. Like the present in the encounter with God, and unlike in its full liberation as a reality.

Index